Reflections from the Soul

Endorsements

I wish I had a copy of this book when I lost my thirty-nine year-old son to an accidental drowning. I was shattered by the loss and felt I had to be everyone else's rock. Looking back, I can see how valuable it would have been to have had this journal to guide me through my grief. Dr. Green's soft, encouraging words would have been just the right touch to help me find my future by communing with those around me instead of greedily keeping my grief to myself. I highly recommend this book to anyone who is facing a loss. Rather than tell you what to do, *Reflections from the Soul* guides you toward finding yourself. It is a wonderful book.

Susan Archibald, PhD
Academic Department Chair, Kaplan University
Author of the Dissertation Study: A Study of Grief Issues in Grandparents Raising Grandchildren

When living the odyssey of life, all people can experience a broken soul when losing a loved one because death is the incurable final chapter in the book of life. When searching for the framework of cathartic grief recovery, I highly recommend Dr. Eboni Ivory Green's book *Reflections from the Soul*, so the therapeutic recovery steps seem shorter rather than longer when walking on a recovery road and redefining your inner self.

I've had the pleasure of working with Dr. Green on several grief topics and I invite you to explore her wisdom to benefit from practical alternatives when overcoming the challenges of grief. Dr. Green's insights inspire an acknowledgement that the final chapter of death is the beginning of one's immortal existence.

Rob McClenahan
Social Media Specialist
www.rightathome.net

As president of the International Caregivers Association, I know firsthand the meaning of loss. I hear about the sadness of losing a close spouse or close family member to Alzheimer's/dementia on a daily basis. Grief from losing a loved one is never easy. Much comfort and encouragement can be gained by reading this book. Answering the questions will help readers to achieve clarity so they can move on. Finally, this book helps readers to realize that although death takes your loved one away, death cannot take the loving memories the person has left behind. Those memories are stored in your heart.

E'thelle G. Lord, DM
International Caregivers Association, LLC

Amazing! I am in awe of how eloquently Dr. Green expresses the feelings we all have when losing a loved one. I especially love the steps, acknowledge your feelings, be inspired, and reflect deeply so that you can heal (AIR). Reflecting upon them and putting the steps into practice will help my soul gain confidence to move forward toward an enriched life.

Carol Marak
Elder Orphan Advocate and Editor at Seniorcare.com

Reflections from the Soul

Dr. Eboni Ivory Green

Foreword by Catrice M. Jackson

Reflections from the Soul

Copyright © 2010-2016 Eboni I. Green.

All rights reserved. No part of this book may be reproduced in any form without permission in writing from the author or publisher.

Green Publishing, PO Box 4291, Omaha, NE 68104

Printed in the United States of America

The information contained in this book is for general informational purposes and is not designed to take the place of the professional advice of a doctor, lawyer, or any other health care professional. Additional caregiving consultation for your individual caregiving situation can be accessed by contacting:

Caregiver Support Services via e-mail at:
caregiversupport@aol.com or by visiting us on the Web at
http://www.caregiversupportservices.org.

ISBN: 978-0-9715582-3-6

Acknowledgments

> *To make the journey and not fall deeply in love—*
> *well, you haven't lived a life at all.*
>
> —Meet Joe Black *(1998)*

I want to take a moment to acknowledge the village of family and close friends who have supported me throughout my life. More importantly, I want to highlight their collective sacrifices and their willingness to share their personal experiences of grief with me.

My husband and soul mate, Terrence, has always been my biggest supporter, collaborator, editor, friend, and confidant. He challenges me to do my best every day, and I am so very thankful for his love and support. Together we share four children, Asia, Tre,' Jordan, and Terryn, and three grandchildren, Sa'Nya, Jayshawn, and Journey, whom we love dearly. In fact, just seeing one of their faces warms my soul.

To my parents, Jose and Laura Torres-Reyes, thank you for always believing in me and having my back no matter what. I want to acknowledge that my stepmom Laura recently lost her father, Robert Eugene Nickerson, after a long battle with Alzheimer's, and I hope that she is surrounded with love and compassion. Laura has been a constant and reliable mentor and friend. In looking at the loving relationship that we share, I am thankful that she had such a wonderful upbringing. I am forever grateful because she has always accepted me with open arms.

I would be remiss if I did not share the deep connection and love lavished upon me by my father, Jose, and his mother, my grandmother, Anna Torres-Reyes. She was statuesque and always made me feel like I was in the presence of a movie star. She lavished me with affection and ignited my love of the Puerto Rican culture. She had BIG love for her family!!! The last time I saw her, we were attending my cousin's wedding. She was well over 70, but I believe she would have still given Raquel Welch a run for her money.

To my mother, Debra, and sister Shayna, I love you!

To my father, Geames Ivory, thank you for your wisdom, for bringing Doris into my life, for caring for my sister Rochelle, and for filling the gap for my niece and nephews who lost their mother.

To my uncle Melvin Hardgraves, Alzheimer's is a terrible disease. Thank you and your family for all you did to care for Gran. I am forever grateful!

Doresa, my sister/cousin with whom I spoke every day while writing this book, you know what your love and support mean to me. To my cousin Cynthia, thank you for being my friend.

Thank you to my cousin Catrice Jackson for writing the foreword and for your loving tribute to our grandmother, Gran.

To my extended family, Ella Mae, Emma, Nikki, Matthew, and Dave, we would not have made it through such challenging times without one another. Thanks for all the hugs and prayers.

I have never met a stronger or more loving person than Me'chelle. I want to acknowledge her wisdom and strength following the recent loss of her daughter Kee'Doria Coleman.

To my best friend, Bridgett, the inspiration for the opening chapter, "Riptides to Land," in honor of her only child, Joe, whom we all love and miss: thank you for demonstrating wisdom and kindness despite your loss. I love you!

To my nieces Shaquita and Dominque I am so proud of the beautiful ladies that you have become.

Thanks to all my aunts, uncles, and friends who were not mentioned by name. Also, thanks to all my family, friends, and caregivers who assisted with the writing process and who have provided continuous care and support.

Of greater importance, thank you, God, for revealing what is most important in my life—family!

Table of Contents

Endorsements iii
Acknowledgments vii
Foreword xiii
Introduction 1

Part One: Life Imprints

Do That Which You Think You Cannot! 7
From Isolation to Communion 11
Little Paper Boats 17
A Quiet Mind 23
The Caretaker of Memories 29
You've Committed No Offense by Surviving 35
The Transfer of Hope 41
The Seven Spiritual Gs 47

Part Two: Reflections for your Soul

Four Questions to Frame Your Pilgrimage 57
Take a Whack at Ouiser 65
Cultivating Life-Enhancing Spirituality 73

The Grace to Grieve 81
Living Without Guilt or Regret? 87
Work by Day and Sleep at Night? 93
Heavy Raindrops 101
Remembering You Makes Me Smile 107
You Do Not Need to Walk Alone 115
Being Mindful 121
The Empty Chair Prayer 129
The Myth of Closure 139
Everyone Hurts 151

Part Three: What About Your Grieving Family?

God Sets the Lonely in Families 147
Everyone Hurts 151

Epilogue: All in Good Time

Dancing Beautifully with a Limp 165

About the Author 171

Foreword

by Catrice M. Jackson, MS, LMHP, LPC

There is a sacredness in tears. They are not the mark of weakness, but of power. They speak more eloquently than ten thousand tongues. They are the messengers of overwhelming grief, of deep contrition, and of unspeakable love.

— Washington Irving[1]

Every spring a distinct, delightful, and familiar fragrance enveloped her home. The subtle aroma of gorgeous lilacs welcomed me every time I reached to open the chain-link gate that my grandfather would have a fit about being left open. The floral invitation was the scent of solace, because I knew I was coming *home* again. Beautiful blooming hues of flowers danced in the flower beds she so passionately loved. She loved gladiolas, irises, and roses and spent many hours planting, pruning, and caring for her botanical babies.

If I close my eyes, I can effortlessly see her bent over digging in the dirt, moving and shifting flowers around as she created a magnificent mosaic that greeted everyone who entered the gate. Reminiscing these moments makes my eyes swell with tears. I weep, for I long to see her again. The fragrance of lilacs followed me and caressed my soul with every eager step toward the side door. Sometimes I walked slowly to savor the heartwarming scent and other times I skipped quickly to the side door with anticipation to enter.

I clearly remember these moments going to my grandmother's house or Gran as we called her. The place where we were allowed to be *free*. The place where the scent of fried chicken, hot water cornbread, and banana pudding were frequent childhood experiences. The place where we laughed until we nearly wet our pants. The place where we played, prayed, and learned about God. The place I called home away from home.

I remember playing school in the kitchen, practicing church songs for the choir in the dining room, and watching Saturday morning cartoons in the living room. I watched my Gran get dressed for church in her bedroom and was mesmerized by all her beautiful jewelry. I remember sleeping on a pallet on the floor in the den as she slept on the couch. I can see myself running, laughing, and playing in every room of her two-story home.

My Gran was a sassy, loving, no-nonsense, God-fearing woman who loved to laugh. I learned so much from her. She taught me how to pray, how to cook and even how to drive. She was feisty, quick-witted, and loved to travel. I have fond memories of us grandkids loading up in "the van" and traveling to various cities for church conventions. I remember peacefully falling asleep on her lap many nights after a long day of church services and revivals. I know God because of my Gran.

In the late 1990s her husband, my grandfather, passed away and things quickly changed. Even though they argued like Fred Sanford and Aunt Esther from *Sanford and Son*, Gran loved and missed my grandfather. She stayed in her home alone for some years and then her health and vitality began to dissipate. Eventually, my uncle, her youngest son moved in with her and the home away from home became a very unfamiliar place.

My Gran was particular about her home. As a homemaker, taking care of her home meant *everything* to her. Slowly everything that reminded us of her was taken down, put away, and thrown out. The walls were empty of all the family photos. Finally, the inside of Gran's home was no longer reminiscent of *her* presence and she was moved into the den to live. Gran once graced each room of her lovely two-bedroom home and now anything she had left was tucked away in one room. I have to admit, walking into her house and seeing her living in a single room made me deeply sad. I didn't understand. It should have been different.

I lived about an hour away from Gran in another city, and every chance I got, I would go visit her. I would bring Gran gifts, snacks, and treats she wasn't "supposed" to have, and I would pluck the hairs from her chin and do her hair. I wanted Gran to feel cared for. She always cared for her hair; it was so important to her. One time while my uncle needed to do some repairs in Gran's living space, she came to stay with me for a week. It was then I really saw how much she had slowed down and needed care.

I bathed her, cooked for her, talked with her. Gran ate dinner *with* us instead of alone in her home's den. I remember Gran waking up in the middle of the night and going into my teenage son's room saying she was hungry. She knew *who* she was with, but, she didn't know *where* she was. The early stages of Alzheimer's were kicking in, but one thing is for sure; my Gran *always* knew who I was, she never forgot me or my son.

After staying with us for a week, Gran returned to her living space. More and more she forgot. She always remembered a handful of people, but, most others she stared at for a while until she remembered or asked who they were. One thing she *never* forgot was how to be sassy and feisty and laugh. She loved to laugh!

In February 2010, we got the call that Gran had been hospitalized and was not responsive. We immediately drove to see her. I walked into Gran's hospital room to see her lifeless body almost frozen still with very little signs of life. She was barely breathing and the death rattle was increasing. We knew it wouldn't be long. I snuggled in the hospital bed beside Gran, stroking her face and hair and peacefully enjoying my *last* moment with her.

I whispered in her ear, "*Its okay, Gran, you can go now. We love you.*" And then, the most divine thing happened. A single tear rolled down her cheek. Gran heard me! She knew I was there! This was the *only* bodily response she displayed for hours prior to our arrival. Within the hour, Gran took her last precious breath. A part of me died with her.

My Gran is physically gone, but very much vibrantly alive within me and those of us who loved her so. I miss her. When I see beautiful flowers I think of Gran. Every time I pass a lilac bush I feel her presence. No one will ever make banana pudding like my Gran. She was my laughing buddy, my keeper, my second mother, my spiritual teacher; she was our matriarch. We've all grieved her passing in our own unique way. There's no right or wrong way; it's always *your* way, the way that feels *right* for you. There's nothing wrong with holding on to the memories or expressing sadness when thoughts of your loved one resurface. Death may have stolen my Gran, but the imprint of her love remains.

Dr. Green shares in *Reflections from the Soul* how linking objects helps us stay connected to our loved ones. What brilliant advice! When I want to be with my Gran I wrap up in one of her favorite quilts and picture her holding me. It takes me home again. As a licensed mental health practitioner and licensed professional counselor, I strongly encourage you to read and apply the essential sage in Dr. Green's message to experience deep, emotional healing and enhance your mental wellness. She transparently shares her own personal stories of not only surviving grief but also offers practical and effective strategies for thriving after loss.

Grief is a personal and unique journey with an often unpredictable destination. Losing someone you love is a deep loss, but, it can also become an everlasting legacy of your love for each other. *Reflections from the Soul* is beautifully and intimately written by a woman who loves people with a big caregiver's heart. Dr. Green message provides you an anchor in the storm of grief, sunshine for the cloudy days ahead, and healing balm for your soul's journey. Her wisdom, words, advice, and strategies are a compassionate compass for navigating through the experience of grief and loss, sprinkled with benevolent drops of hope, restoration, and refreshment to reignite your joy on the journey.

Catrice M. Jackson, MS, LMHP, LPC
International Speaker, Best-Selling Author,
Mental Wellness Mentor
www.catriceologyenterprises.com

---

[1] Washington Irving, BrainyQuote, (Xplore, Inc, 2016). http://www.brainyquote.com/quotes/quotes/w/washington149294.html, accessed September 21, 2016.

Introduction

Matters of the heart are never truly closed. The sadness associated with losing someone you love never goes away completely. Yet, there is hope that one day the deep sorrow will now take a place in history.

—Dr. Eboni Ivory Green

Survival Breath

Imagine that you are sailing in open water on your way to a beautiful island. You have been traveling for a long time, but you finally catch a glimpse of the island off in the distance and feel a sense of relief that you are so close to reaching your destination. You take this opportunity to bask in the sun as it shines brightly and you listen to the music of the waves as they ripple against the sides of your boat.

Just when you feel totally relaxed, a substantial wave pummels you, forcing you to grip the boat tightly until the swell passes. The surging water leaves you shaken, so you take a moment and collect yourself as you acknowledge that the smoothness of a boat ride in open water often depends on elements that are not within your control.

As you begin to recover from the wave force, a riptide crashes in and thrusts you from the safety of your boat. You take a deep breath, known as a survival breath, and sink underwater until the riptide passes and you have the opportunity to bob to the surface. As you break through the water's surface, you release the air you were holding in your lungs. After several moments, you catch your breath and find that you are breathing normally again. You spot the distant island and it is much closer than you previously thought. It is evident that you are going to make it to land! You swim the short distance to the island and nearly collapse in sheer relief.

Riptides of Sadness

The sadness associated with grief can be analogous to being hurled out of the safety of a boat by a riptide. A riptide, or a current opposing another current, may also equate to the turmoil and inner conflict you feel when you lose a loved one for whom you have cared. Just as you might feel helpless against the elemental sea when being heaved from a boat, you will likely be emotionally fragile when your loved one dies. In fact, you may feel that you will be swept away by your grief. As in the boat analogy, you may feel as though you are underwater, gasping to catch your breath, and with so many competing emotions; from time to time, you may even feel as though you are going to go crazy. I would bet that you will not.

Faced with such deep and raw emotions, there are generally two approaches to coping. The first is to shut down and bury your feelings deep within. However, burying your feelings is not a healthy approach to coping with grief. Over time, suppressed feelings often resurface and could result in increased anxiety or clinical depression.

The second approach is to dig deep to garner your inner strength and work to address your feelings of sadness. I hope you will dig deep, embrace your inner strength, and do the tough work associated with working through grief. Ultimately, as you experience the emotions associated with losing someone you love, your survival skills will take over and you will recognize the importance of resisting the temptation to fight the waves of sadness that you will undoubtedly experience at times. And you will learn to embrace your raw emotions.

This is why the surviving the tossed overboard analogy is so important—because reaching the *island* means that you are getting back to a sense of you and reaching some level of homeostasis with the sadness you presently feel.

Closure?

It should be noted that reaching homeostasis is different from closure. The term *closure* captures a mythological tidiness that most of us will not achieve in our grief. The truth is that losing a loved one changes your life forever, and though you will likely not get over your sadness, it is possible to learn to cope. Therefore, it is important to be cautious of the suggestion that the goal of grief work is to find closure, that you should only experience sadness briefly, and that you will then close the door on your sadness and return to normal. This is simply not true. Loss changes you.

Healthy Ways to Express Your Sadness

Because you will be changed by your loss, it is important to identify strategies that may be useful in expressing your sadness. The ultimate goal of each of the approaches is to help you begin to integrate your past and present feelings about your loved one so that you are able to invest your emotions into living.

Poetry. Writing poetry was one of the ways I coped when my aunt Linda passed away. I would find myself awake in the middle of the night without anyone with whom I could express my sadness, and so I would write. The key to successful poetry writing as an outlet to expressing your sadness is that it does not have to be nicely written, spelled correctly, or even flow succinctly. What matters is that you fully express yourself and have an opportunity to capture how you are feeling in the moment.

Many of the poems I wrote after my aunt passed away have never been shared with anyone. In fact, the journal is tucked away and serves as a private tribute to our special relationship. It is up to you what you do with your written words long term. For now, the goal is to release your feelings in a healthy manner.

Life Imprint. Cynthia was my favorite aunt; she had a magnetic personality and loved to laugh. When she passed away after a long struggle with a bipolar disorder, I wasn't sure how I would cope with the sadness. Yet, having time to reflect helped me recognize that we continue to have a relationship, because, through her humor, she left a strong life imprint. Remembering her makes me smile. I try to be mindful that I have not lost the years caring for her. Rather, I try to incorporate new patterns of living that include the transformed but abiding relationship that still exists. I have concluded that I am a living memorial of my aunt.

Linking Objects. There is an afghan blanket that holds a special place in my heart. My children know about the blanket and that it is my grandmother's. What they don't know is how seeing one of them wrapped in the blanket brings me joy. Linking objects like the afghan blanket can be a healthy way of honoring your loved one. What helps me make it through on some of the most difficult days is keeping the memory of my grandmother Frankie alive by incorporating into our daily lives something that she loved.

As mentioned previously, I do not believe that one is likely to ever get over the death of a loved one. What I do believe is that we learn to incorporate the best attributes of our departed loved ones into our daily lives. We remember what we loved best about them. Our lives are forever changed from knowing those who are now gone, and the beauty of loss is that one day we will see them again.

Part One: Life Imprints

*Death leaves a heartache no one can heal,
love leaves and imprint no one can steal.*

-Adapted from an Irish headstone

Do That Which You Think You Cannot!

We gain strength, and courage, and confidence by each experience in which we really stop to look fear in the face. . . . We must do that which we think we cannot.

—Eleanor Roosevelt[1]

Some individuals are born knowing life's purpose. They embrace their destiny and work steadily, if not methodically, until they achieve their goals. For others, the path to greatness is not as clear; their journeys are met with challenges that must be overcome, and it is only after experiencing the pain of loss that their divine providence is revealed.

Eleanor Roosevelt is an example of the latter. As a young girl, she experienced the pain of loss in quick succession. Between 1892 and 1894, Eleanor's mother, younger brother, and father died, leaving her and her brother to be raised by their grandmother. Eleanor grew up feeling disconnected, lonely, and withdrawn and she longed for affection. At the age of nineteen, she met, fell in love with, and married Franklin Delano Roosevelt. Together the couple had six children but tragically lost their third child, an infant son named Franklin. The roles of wife, mother, and daughter meant a great deal to Eleanor, yet her mother-in-law, Sara Roosevelt, proved to be an overbearing force who undermined Eleanor's efforts with the children and the home.

In 1921, Eleanor's husband was stricken with polio. His diagnosis not only left him paralyzed from the waist down, but also appeared it would derail his political career as well. It took Eleanor's quiet confidence to encourage her husband, who was fiercely independent, to follow his path to greatness despite his physical condition. It is evident she applied her famous uncle Theodore's advice to "speak softly and carry a big stick and you will go far."

Although Franklin never conceded that his condition was permanent, the pair opened themselves to a new consciousness in their relationship and worked collaboratively for the good of the two and, ultimately, the country. They modeled the *Power of Two*, a principle common among caregivers that is biblically based and introduced in my second book, *At the Heart of the Matter*: "two are better than one; because they have a good reward for their labor. For if they fall, the one will lift up his fellow."[2]

Eleanor redefined her role as a wife and caregiver, and as a result, Franklin came to depend on her a great deal for the rest of his life. As first lady, Eleanor was admired at home and abroad for her empathy for the disadvantaged. Yet one of her most meaningful contributions to society occurred following the death of her husband. Eleanor was instrumental in seeing the Universal Declaration of Human Rights of 1948 adopted as an internationally recognized proclamation.

Eleanor faced a great many losses in her life. Her marriage was not perfect, nor were some of her interpersonal relationships, including the relationships with her children. She was a very private person, yet much of the grief she experienced in her private life was known to the public. This loss of private grief deeply distressed Eleanor. Yet, she is just one example of what is possible when caregivers face their sadness and redirect their feelings of grief.

Although no two people will respond exactly in the same way to loss, Eleanor seems to have relied on her faith, deep reflection, and meaningful introspection to carve out a legacy that continues to add richness to the lives of millions.

For this reason, *Reflections from the Soul* uses a historical lens to tell a story of a different person, famous or otherwise, who has cared for and lost a loved one but who also used pain as an agent for healing. As C. JoyBell C. states:

> Pain is a pesky part of being human, I've learned it feels like a stab wound to the heart, something I wish we could all do without, in our lives here. Pain is a sudden hurt that can't be escaped. But then I have also learned that because of pain, I can feel the beauty, tenderness, and freedom of healing. Pain feels like a fast stab wound to the heart. But then healing feels like the wind against your face when you are spreading your wings and flying through the air! We may not have wings growing out of our backs, but healing is the closest thing that will give us that wind against our faces.[3]

It is my hope that in sharing these stories and strategies, this book will provide a road map for coping and will in some small way encourage you to work through your sadness. I pray that you stay open to doing that which you think you cannot by opening your heart so that your soul can heal.

---

[1] Eleanor Roosevelt, By Instilling Resilience, Confidence, and Grit, According to Recent Research by McKinsey, Based on Interview Data with 250 Senior Executive Women. "9 Quotes: Inspire a Thriving Culture | Executive Coaching Connections." 9 Quotes: Inspire a Thriving Culture | Executive Coaching Connections. Accessed September 21, 2016. http://www.executivecoachingconnections.com/discover/9-quotes-inspire-thriving-culture#sthash.0kB5ogRW.dpuf.

[2] Thomas Nelson, *The NKJV Study Bible*, 2nd ed. (Nashville: Harper Publishing, 2007), Ecclesiastes 4:9–10.

[3] C. JoyBell C., *Goodreads* (Goodreads Inc., 2006), http://www.goodreads.com/quotes/396855-pain-is-a-pesky-part-of-being-human-i-ve-learned,.accessed September 21, 2016.

From Isolation to Communion

I understand that allowing the full reality of this death to enter my head and heart is a source of necessary hurt. While I do not seek the hurt, I seek the healing. Once I understand that the pain actually begins to dissolve. Yes, I still hurt, but the depth of the pain will ease over time.

—Allen Wolfelt[1]

In the movie *Meet Joe Black*[2], a Jamacian woman (actress Lois Kelly-Miller) is coping with excruciating pain from a terminal disease. She clearly explains the loneliness all humans experience when she tells Joe Black (actor Brad Pitt) that people are mostly lonely—a fact that grieving caregivers know all too well. Yet for those who are blessed to commune with family and friends, the mental pictures carried throughout life both while your loved one is living and after he or she has passed have the ability to influence your life in ways that are both positive and meaningful.

Many caregivers coping with loss not only experience a period of loneliness but also can become socially and emotionally isolated. While sharing your memories alone will not shield you from experiencing loneliness and isolation, reaching out to create new ones can make a difference in how you process your grief.

ISOLATION, LONELINESS, AND SOLITUDE: IS THERE A DIFFERENCE?

Isolation

Isolation is usually a gradual change in relationships where there is a loss of contact with once close family and friends until you find that you are having little or no contact with individuals who were a part of your inner circle. The loss of connection may result in feelings of disconnection and loneliness.

Loneliness

Loneliness by definition relates to how you feel when your social network becomes smaller than desired. In some instances, the size of your social network is impacted by geographical separation, as you may simply be too far away to feel connected to family and friends. In other instances, your family members might be living in the same city, yet you find it difficult to get together simply because your lives are jam-packed with responsibilities and commitments. The result is that even when you are supportive of one another, you may still feel a sense of loneliness.

You also might begin to experience increased loneliness when you come to realize that when you lose someone you love, you lose not only the person but also the hopes and dreams you had for the future—which really hurts and can further contribute to your feelings of loneliness.

Solitude

It should be noted that there is a difference between isolation, loneliness, and solitude. Solitude can be viewed as a form of self-preservation, whereas isolation and loneliness are more or less imposed. Solitude, or alone time to process your grief, is necessary for your health and well-being and coping, so that you have time to emotionally face the overwhelming feelings associated with the death of your loved one.

When you are seeking solitude, you may find that you have withdrawn from family and friends because you are not ready to commune. In fact, you may feel as though you might be overcome by your emotions or wonder how you are going to cope if you allow yourself to acknowledge everything that you are feeling right now.

It is important to take advantage of alone time. However, if you find that you are isolated and lonely, then you are more than likely experiencing something altogether different than simply taking time for yourself. In fact, isolation and loneliness are unhealthy responses that, left unchecked, can negatively impact your health and well-being. Isolation and loneliness among caregivers are associated with increased mortality, depression, physical health problems, and other health-related issues.

All of this leads to the question: is there a duty to commune with family and friends following the loss of your loved one? If so, is the duty not only for your healing but also for the healing of your living family members? I would say that the answer is yes.

WHAT EXACTLY IS COMMUNION AND HOW DOES IT HELP WITH PROCESSING GRIEF?

The term *communion* is usually thought of in religious terms, for example, when one takes communion at church. However, when coping with your grief, communion involves talking together intimately and in close rapport to support one another after a loved one passes. Communion is a spiritual sharing of the mental pictures and memories carried from the time spent with your loved one who is now passed. Sharing these memories with family and friends can aid you in expressing your grief in a positive manner. Communion is not simply about surrounding yourself with people, rather, it is about sharing your experience and opening yourself to new ones.

My mother is a testament to the importance of communion to prevent isolation and loneliness. With the passing of my grandmother and then my two aunts (first my aunt Linda and, more recently, my aunt Cynthia), my mother instantly became a matriarch. She was the youngest of her siblings and had cared for my grandmother and aunts. Just like many caregivers coping with loss, my mother felt a sense of duty to hold the family together, and as a result, she did not have time to process her grief.

Over time, she shut down and became both lonely and isolated. It was like she lost her entire support system in a brief period of time and she wasn't able to talk to anyone about her loss because she hurt so deeply. In fact, most people would say that she was uncharacteristically resilient, because no one knew that she felt so alone.

This is why it is important to share, because some might think you are displaying a level of calm or patience, and they may even compliment you on your unwavering strength. Others might wonder how you made it through all that you have up to that point, when the truth is that you have completely cut yourself off from your feelings.

When you experience isolation, you may have supportive family and friends who are readily available to share in your pain, yet you find that you cannot be around family members because it reminds you of your grief. The truth is that everyone has a different way of processing his or her feelings. However, no one knows how you feel unless you are willing to share your feelings.

How to avoid isolation and loneliness

Remember that if you are feeling lonely or isolated, others in your social circle likely feel the same. Keep in mind the words of the Jamaican woman in *Meet Joe Black*: that most people are mostly lonely, and this is why communion is so important. To enhance your ability to commune, you might consider building on existing interpersonal relationships among family, but do not stop there—be sure to socialize with friends from work and your community. Building a diverse social network including a variety of meaningful relationships outside of family members is important.

Also remember that the activities in which you participate are not only a part of who you are but also will aid you in coping with the stress of losing someone you love. Finally, communion is all about guiding one another through feelings of grief rather than forcing people to express feelings. Therefore, time for reflection is equally important when you are seeking to avoid isolation and loneliness following the loss of a loved one.

---

[1] Wolfelt, Alan. *The Journey through Grief: Reflections on Healing.* Fort Collins, CO: Companion Press, 1997.

[2] Bo Goldman, Keven Wade, Jeff Reno, Ron Osbom. *Meet Joe Black*, directed by Martin Best (United States: Universal Studios, 1998).

Little Paper Boats

A void in my chest was beginning to fill with anger. Quiet, defeated anger that guaranteed me the right to my hurt that believed no one could possibly understand that hurt.

—Rachel Sontag[1]

My aunt Linda was sick all her life. When she was young, she began suffering from an inflammatory bowel disorder. Although it was many years later that a formal diagnosis of Crohn's was made, she suffered immensely from the devastating effects of the disease for most of her life. Aunt Linda was determined to live a full life despite her disease, so she joined and later retired from the U.S. Marines.

A few years after retiring, Aunt Linda began experiencing excruciating pain from boils under her arms, and despite taking a prescription, when one boil healed, another would appear. She confided in my grandmother, a registered nurse, about the reoccurring boils. My grandmother insisted that my aunt see the doctor immediately. When the test results came back from the doctor, Aunt Linda was diagnosed with leukemia. We were all devastated; however, once she received treatment, the leukemia went into remission.

One evening a few years later, my mother and I were catching up when she mentioned that Aunt Linda, who had had no menstruation since undergoing chemotherapy for leukemia more than five years earlier, had started menstruating and had not stopped in three months. My heart dropped. I told my mother that it was not normal to start your menstrual cycle after five years and that constant bleeding in any case should be evaluated immediately. I spoke with my aunt briefly and encouraged her to go to the doctor. When I did not hear anything more, I was comforted.

Later that summer, her twins graduated from high school, and Aunt Linda put her house up for sale, retired from her part-time job, and relocated to Arizona. During the Christmas holiday, my mom called and said she was on her way to visit my aunt who was in the hospital. Since Aunt Linda had relocated in the summer, the bleeding had continued and she was in constant pain and short of breath. Every symptom she described was a classic symptom of ovarian cancer: the pelvic or abdominal pain, the extra fluid in the abdomen, and the abnormal menstrual cycles.

By the time Aunt Linda was admitted to the hospital, the ovarian tumor was the size of a football. Her prognosis was poor, and the doctors said she only had days to live. She was released from the hospital and taken home to be cared for by her husband and children. On the morning of January 2, 2007, Aunt Linda died.

I was so angry when she died. The anguish I experienced was an impending storm brewing in my heart. Oh, how the agony would move swiftly through my soul just how storms rapidly approach the coastline. For some time after my aunt Linda died, I couldn't cry because I felt such anger. Later, when I did feel like crying, my tears were replaced with an overwhelming sense of frustration and resentment so that I would start to cry, but the tears would not fall. I was angry that she got so sick so fast, that my mom lost her best friend, and that I wanted to be there for Aunt Linda but couldn't make it in time. Later I realized that my anger was only masking how deeply I was hurting.

I do not think that I shared my anger with anyone other than my husband, and even he did not understand the extent of my feelings. For the next few years, I remained angry about my aunt's death.

When something in my life was upsetting, I could feel the rage about my aunt's death creep in; however, I would quickly find something on which to focus to avoid addressing my anger.

ARE YOU ANGRY?

Anger is a companion to grief. In fact, it is not uncommon to feel vulnerable, frustrated, and angry following the loss of your loved one. When it comes to the source of anger among grieving caregivers, you might be surprised to know that most anger results from unresolved feelings within the family, feelings of guilt about what should have or could have been done to care for your loved one, and a sense of a loss of control over life and death. The anger you feel can be intense, or you may find that you are caught unaware.

The truth is it is okay to be angry. A certain amount of anger following the loss of your loved one is considered healthy. However, when you are angry for an extended period of time, or lack sufficient coping and problem-solving skills, you are more likely to experience complicated grief.

Complicated grief is a persistant response to losing a loved one, lasting six months or longer, with a general disengagement from participation in normal everyday life activities. I recently spoke with a caregiver who was experiencing complicated grief following the loss of her husband. As we talked, she expressed feelings of sadness related to his death, which she revealed had happened some time ago. She also admitted that she suppressed her feelings of grief and instead focused her energy on what she termed the endless needs of her adult sons, and as a result, she was very angry.

Complicated grief is by nature multifarious because your emotions are often jumbled. For example, you may feel frustrated, numb, attached, and distant all at the same time, which can be very difficult to gauge and understand. The caregiver in the example recognized she was emotionally compromised by her anger, and after we talked, she sought counseling and treatment to move forward.

Although the type of anger that you experience while you are grieving usually does not preclude you from experiencing positive feelings, when anger is poorly managed, it can be distancing and lead to participation in unhealthy behaviors. If you find that you are constantly angry, it is important that you work to identify the deeper meaning behind your feelings. Constant anger may be a warning sign that you have unresolved feelings and that you are not fully absorbing the loss or giving yourself permission to fully grieve your loss.

Working through Anger

There is not much to go on when it comes to how caregivers can work through the anger associated with grief. Relatively few studies, scales, or assessments evaluate anger among grieving caregivers. What we do know is that anger can be useful when explored and thoughtfully addressed. The following are three suggestions for healthy ways to cope with anger: (1) discharging emotional residue, (2) leaning on your social network, and (3) avoid using aggressive anger management techniques.

Release the emotional residue. An important step in regaining a sense of well-being is giving yourself permission to release the emotional residue that is attached to the death of your loved one. The truth is that you may have been immersed in caring for your loved one and in turn have not had an opportunity to fully express your sadness or anger. It is essential to understand that you might have to work up to fully expressing your sadness and that a failure to release your feelings of anger often manifests in unhealthy behaviors. One strategy that caregivers find useful is to vent about resentments that may have resulted from caring for a loved one who was quite ill. This includes voicing the challenges faced with the loved one's illness and the sadness associated with his or her death.

While the emotion of anger will likely not be released simply by venting bottled up emotional responses, verbal expression and being heard and understood by an empathetic listener, can play a significant role in helping you finish the business of reducing the feeling of anger associated with the death of your loved one. Just having the opportunity to have your feelings validated can be very helpful.

It is vital to note the importance of being careful with venting as, in some situations, it can increase your anger. In fact, remembering and sharing certain events aloud can increase your feelings of anger rather than decrease them. Simply put, emotional expression does not automatically lead to anger reduction.

Be sure to express your need for support. Having access to your family and friends for support can restore a sense of balance as other family members may also be feeling distressed or angry. Sharing thoughts and emotions and being understood by family and friends in an empathetic manner is by far what caregivers find the most comforting and important. An informal method to practice empathic listening is having each family member read a letter expressing his or her feelings of sadness.

Once the letter is written, you might try reading the letter aloud as it can be helpful to express your anger with listeners who are empathetic. Working through your anger is best facilitated with effective communication techniques. If you are communicating your feelings with your family and friends, you are developing a strong basis for social support and an outlet to express your anger.

Shy away from participating in aggressive anger management techniques. It is not a good idea to participate in aggressive behaviors like yelling, breaking a glass, or punching a pillow when you are angry. Aggressive anger management techniques only serve to make caregivers feel angrier. If you are angry, stepping away for a few moments can defuse the situation. If feelings of anger persist, it might be a good idea to speak with a licensed health professional, so that you have the opportunity to work through your anger.

Just like stress, anger gets a bad rap, when in fact it can serve you well in some situations. However, if your anger is not harnessed properly, the emotional implications can be far-reaching. My healing only occurred once I was able to acknowledge the source of my anger.

I had to openly accept that I would not ever be able to make sense out of my aunt Linda's suffering. I am not as angry, but there are times when I am overcome by my feelings and I continue to take small measured steps to release my anger. For example, when I sense the anger getting the best of me, I listen to classical music. I particularly appreciate melodies without words as it calms my nerves and eases my distress. Should you find that you are angry, please take the time to get the support you need to manage your anger so that you can avoid experiencing complicated grief.

---

[1] Rachel Sontag, Goodreads, (Goodreads Inc., 2006). http://www.goodreads.com/quotes/248996-a-void-in-my-chest-was-beginning-to-fill-with,.accessed September 21, 2016.

A Quiet Mind

The Means to Attain a Happy Life

Martial the things that do attain
The happy life be these, I find:—
The riches left, not got with pain;
The fruitful ground, the quiet mind;

The equal friend; no grudge, no strife;
No charge of rule, nor governance;
Without disease, the healthful life;
The household of continuance;

The mean diet, no delicate fare;
True wisdom joined with simplicity;
The night discharged of all care,
Where wine the wit may not oppress.

The faithful wife, without debate;
such sleeps as may beguile the night:
Contented with thine own estate
Ne wish for death, ne fear his might.

—Henry Howard, Earl of Surrey[1]

Mary Todd Lincoln led a privileged and unfortunate life. Born into a wealthy family, she wanted for nothing material, yet her emotional state was something altogether different. In a constant state of distress, Mary was plagued by anxiety and suffered through bouts of intense melancholy. Most of Mary's pain stemmed from the untimely death of her mother who died when Mary was just seven. But Mary's pain continued through her young life as she was ignored by her father and did not care for her stepmother.

When Mary married Abraham Lincoln, she intended their union to be a safe haven and vowed that her children would grow up in a loving and nurturing home. Once married, Mary valued her role as a wife and mother above everything in life and kept her promise by indulging her children and lavishing them with love.

Tragically, three of her four sons died before becoming adults. Later, as First Lady of the United States, Mary was in a position of great influence, but she lost all of the prestige, status, and protections when her husband, President Lincoln, was assassinated.

Over the years, Mary's compiling losses served to intensify her melancholy and exaggerate her feelings of anxiety, leaving her isolated to deal with her inconsolable grief. Her lifelong struggle with anxiety does not have to be lost in history; rather, it can serve as a foundation as to how you might recognize these symptoms in your grief.

Mary's Distress

Following President Lincoln's assassination, Mary was extremely distressed, and rightfully so. She was not only coping with her grief but also facing a variety of devastating realities. Her immediate concerns centered on where she would live and how she would provide for her sons, but she was equally concerned with preserving her husband's legacy. Adding to her anguish, most of her relationships were strained so that she did not have anyone with whom she could share her private thoughts. Mary had a lot to worry about.

Recognizing Symptoms of Stress in Grief

Emotional distress is a common response to losing someone you love. In fact, for a time, you will likely feel worried, overwhelmed, restless, and tearful. You may have trouble sleeping and find that you are overeating or undereating.

What Can You Do to Begin Working with Your Distress?

Take the time you need to process your feelings. You will likely have a lot to worry about; therefore it is vital to give yourself permission to take time to process your feelings and, whenever possible, to try to express them as they arise. It is equally important to know that you do not have to be strong for others and that if there ever was a time to express yourself, it is now.

In the long run, you need time to process, to release your emotions, and to lean on your emotional supports. Without proper outlets, you may find that you have unhealthy thoughts rolling around without a way to express them. Try talking to a close friend, a counselor, or your pastor. Over time, expressing your feelings will be better for your personal healing.

Quieting an Anxious Mind

After President Lincoln died, Mary still had her sons Robert and Thomas Lincoln (Tad) to share her grief. Although she was not very close with Robert, she and Tad were able to depend on one another. Mary made special efforts to care for Tad, traveling to find the best treatments for his chewing and swallowing problems. She also invested heavily in his education. Sadly, Tad died following a brief illness at the age of eighteen. In her despair, I am sure that Mary wished to quiet her mind, yet she found that she would never again experience a night discharged from all cares.

Recognizing Symptoms of Anxiety in Grief

Anxiety is an extreme response to grief. Symptoms can include difficulty with concentrating, poor decision-making, and a disruption in your ability to sleep. You may also experience reduced satisfaction in activities you once found enjoyable. In addition, anxiety may cause you to view difficult situations but possible solvable problems as threatening.

What Can You Do to Begin Addressing Your Feelings of Anxiety?

Identify your biggest triggers. It is important to recognize that you may have had little time to adjust to the demands of caring for and then losing someone whom you love. Managing the anxiety associated with having provided care can be complex. It is essential to identify your greatest triggers for anxiety so that while you are healing, you can avoid activities that will only serve to intensify your fears.

Other possible strategies for working through anxiety include meditation, deep breathing, and head-to-toe body relaxation exercises. Some find that listening to calming music or just stepping away from an intense situation for a moment can reduce immediate feelings of anxiety. If you find that your symptoms of anxiety are lasting longer than a few days or that you are feeling panicked, please do not hesitate to reach out to your family physician.

Mary, the Mother of Post-Traumatic Stress

One might not have been able to avoid post-traumatic stress disorder (PTSD) during a time when there was such violence (the Civil War) and loss (a husband and three sons). Although the disorder did not receive formal recognition until 1980, Mary Todd Lincoln could be considered the mother of post-traumatic stress. We know that she suffered from anxiety for much of her life, but losing so much that mattered only served to intensify her anxiety.

Mary began to have irrational fears, and she suffered from nervous exhaustion and panic attacks, during which she would experience chest pain, nausea, headaches, difficulty breathing, and restless wanderings in her night dress; she simply could not be calmed. She played the details of Lincoln's assassination over and over in her mind and was often seized with the conviction that her sole surviving son, Robert, was dying.

Recognizing Symptoms of Post-Traumatic Stress Disorder in Grief

Often associated with veterans of the armed services, PTSD is an anxiety disorder that results when you experience a particularly distressing and traumatic event. It can simply show up after or result from long-term trauma, but it is not usually one thing or another, but a pile up, that results in PTSD. For some time, you may simply feel the tip of the iceberg of your trauma and stress, although there is so much more under the surface.

Increasing evidence suggests that as a grieving caregiver, you are at risk for developing PTSD. You may be at an increased risk for developing PTSD if your loved one has suffered from a life-threatening illness such as cancer, or a long-term debilitating illness such as dementia. Researchers suggest that caring for a sick or disabled loved one with a life-threatening disease may arouse feelings of grief, anger, and sometimes hopelessness, which over time may result in a PTSD response.

There is also evidence that PTSD is prevalent among caregivers who participate in making end-of-life decisions, especially when a loved one subsequently passes away. Caregivers who are experiencing symptoms of PTSD often blame themselves for not being there enough or doing enough for a loved one (even if the feelings are not warranted) and experience feelings of hopelessness, despair, guilt, and/or physical distress. Left untreated, PTSD can negatively impact your psychological well-being.

What If You Think You Are Suffering from PTSD?

Reach out and access sources of support. There are healthy ways to cope with and work through symptoms of PTSD. The first step is recognizing the risks for developing the disorder and then reaching out and accessing sources of support, when needed. Of course, there is no quick fix when it comes to working through PTSD.

Identifying your sources of anxiety and distress is best accomplished by working with a trained health care professional. Most professionals suggest using a combined approach to treating the disorder, including medication, cognitive behavioral therapy, and other therapies to work through the triggers of stress and anxiety. However, it is up to you and your health care professional to determine the strategy that will work best for you.

Also, a variety of general stress management techniques and healthy approaches to living can be effective components of a plan to decrease your stress, anxiety, and symptoms of PTSD. It will take time to find what works best. The key is to continue working with your health care team, family, and other supports until your plan is reflective of your needs so that you can quiet your mind in a way that is both safe and healthy, with the goal being that you continue to live your life with meaning and purpose.

---

[1] Henry Howard, Earl of Surrey, *The Poetical Works of Henry Howard, Earl of Surrey*. (Boston: Little, Brown and Company, 1854), 57.

The Caretaker of Memories

Through sorrows deep her path has led,
and tender ties have sundered been;
Bright hopes were buried with her dead,
and love has kept their memory green.

By grief secluded from the world,
her path through lonely years she trod,
and oft her life has been imperiled;
but she has leaned upon her God.
—Joseph Horatio Chant 1885[1]

Queen Victoria of England began her reign at a relatively young age and, within a couple years of ascending to the throne, married her soul mate and confidant, Prince Albert. However, midway through their life together, the prince developed typhoid fever and died suddenly. Queen Victoria, overcome with grief, was not only said to primarily dress in black for the rest of her life but also became the caretaker of the prince's memory by having his baths drawn, his shaving items prepared, and his clothing ceremonially laid out every morning for the next forty years.

The loss of Prince Albert was significant in a long history of losses that the queen experienced throughout her life, beginning with her father when she was just an infant. In fact, prior to marrying Albert, she seems to have lived in a type of protective isolation. Although she was able to work through her grief-related depression with previous losses, one would be hard-pressed to find examples of where the queen was able enjoy much in life after she lost her husband.

There are few documented cases of individuals suffering such profound depression following the loss of a loved one as what Victoria experienced after losing Prince Albert. Perhaps her grief-related depression was complicated because she did not have the opportunity to care for the prince owing to the brevity of his illness and because those in her court, sensing the potential for distress, chose to keep the truth about his condition quiet.

Queen Victoria's story provides a solid example of what it looks like when you suffer from complicated grief-related depression.

Grief

It is normal to have an emotional response when you experience a significant loss. Most caregivers who are grieving share common feelings, including guilt, emotional release, depression, anger, and isolation. However, grief often comes in waves; you have the ability to maintain the hope that things will get better, and your self-esteem and ability to reach out for assistance (empowerment) are usually present as well.

When you are grieving, you often experience sadness, yet even when you are sad, you have the ability to feel pleasant emotions. Generally you retain the ability to find meaning in your life and, over time, establish a new equilibrium so that you can resume normal activity. Complicated grief that results in depression is something altogether different.

Depression

Losing someone you love can be depressing, which is why depression is often a companion to grief. Yet, there is a discernable difference between what might be considered normal grief and complicated grief-related depression.

For example, when you are experiencing complicated grief-related depression, there is a surrendering of yourself to distress, a general exaggerated hollow feeling often marked by hoplessness, a sense of self-doubt, and a general disengagement from participation in the activities of normal, everyday life.

You may feel that you are in control of your emotions one day and as though you have no control the next. Sometimes you may even feel that you are going to go crazy. Tearfulness, changes in your eating habits, guilt, isolation, fatigue, troubled sleep, and physical symptoms are also possible indicators of complicated grief-related depression. It is not defined by a specific time frame but rather by the continuous, throbbing gloom and doom, all day, every day, like a sad cloud that never goes away.

So how do you know you are experiencing complicated grief-related depression?

You are having outbursts of crying and tearfulness all the time. Crying is a normal part of grief. In fact, you should embrace your tears. Sometimes you may find that you are tearful because you are reflecting, and other times you may simply be crying because you are sad. Over time, with grief, you are usually able to release your emotions through tears. Although you might not feel immediate relief following a good cry, you will find that you are crying less and less as time passes. Should you find that you are crying all the time or that your tears interfere with your ability to participate in normal activities for an extended period of time, you might be experiencing complicated grief-related depression.

You find that you are experiencing changes in your eating habits. A loss of appetite, overeating, undereating, and unintended weight loss could all be indicators of grief initially; however, long-term changes (lasting two weeks or more) could be a symptom of complicated grief-related depression. Remember that eating properly when you are grieving may help you feel better later down the road. Fish oils, shellfish, seafood, eggs, green vegetables, and poultry are suggested natural foods that may help to improve your mood. If you find that you are undereating, try to pick foods that you find appetizing and combine those items to create a meal, as it is common that some foods can seem unappetizing and bland. Eating with others might also work to improve your appetite. Overeating might be another response to grief. You may notice that you are overeating to cope with your loss. If you find that your appetite does not return to normal over time, you may want to speak to your doctor or a nutritionist so that you are able to determine a proper diet.

You find that you are more than just sad. Of course, feeling sad, blue, irritable, or even agitated is normal following the loss of a loved one. However, if you find that you are feeling guilty, worthless, or helpless or are experiencing a diminished quality of life, perhaps you might seek deeper meaning behind your feelings.

Expressing yourself with family members, to trusted members of your church, in general conversation with a close friend, or in a support group may be a healthy way to cope with your sadness. It is important to vent with someone who is a good listener and who will allow you to state your feelings without repercussions. If you do not have someone with whom you can talk in a confidential manner, seeking out a grief counselor is another option. Remember that no matter how you are feeling, you are not a burden to others, as expressing your grief is important to your healing.

You find that you are having trouble sleeping. Many caregivers, especially in the early days of their grief, find that they are having trouble sleeping, which can lead to a confused state of mind, including rambling thoughts. You might find that you are sleeping too much or too little, or that you are still feeling exhausted even when you have had adequate rest, resulting in concentration and memory problems.

Without adequate sleep, it is not possible to heal, as lack of sleep can make it more difficult to summon the energy to combat depression. You need sleep because sleep revitalizes you. If you find that you are having trouble sleeping, it might be important to try natural ways to improve your sleep, for example, using relaxing audiotapes, reorganizing your day so that you are able to wind down, and decreasing your caffeine intake during the day.

Please feel free to refer the chapter "Work by Day and Sleep at Night?" for additional suggestions to combating sleeplessness. Should these strategies fail, it would be important to speak with your doctor.

You find that you are isolating yourself. Decreased ability to socialize at work, school, and otherwise can lead to social isolation over time. If you find that you are socially isolating yourself, it can be helpful to seek opportunities to openly express your feelings to others, acknowledging the reality of your loss.

In the beginning, you might find it easier to attend activities in which you do not have to participate actively but still allow social contact. Identifying what brings joy or meaning to your life and incorporating one or two of these activities into your daily routine is another important step you can take to avoid socially isolating.

You find that you are having physical symptoms. You may find that your symptoms of complicated grief-related depression are manifesting as physical problems, such as headaches, digestive problems, or chronic pain. You may suppress these feelings because you do not want to admit that you feel depressed or because you are not ready to cope with the loss of your loved one. If you find that you are experiencing physical problems, consider that perhaps your symptoms are related to your grief. Talk openly with your doctor or someone whom you trust regarding your physical and emotional symptoms so that you are able to determine if they are related to your grief.

You find that you lack motivation. Lack of motivation, lack of energy, fatigue, and feeling tired are normal for a while following the loss of someone you love. However, if you find that you are lacking motivation all the time, experience a loss of interest in things you once found enjoyable, or stop caring for your physical appearance, you might seek deeper meaning behind your lack of motivation.

You will likely be changed by caring for and losing someone you love. Although, if you find that you are not able to process your grief and are feeling depressed, it is vital that you reach out to someone you trust for assistance. However, if you find that you need professional counseling and care, please do not feel afraid to seek this out.

Fortunately, there have been major improvements in recognizing and treating complicated grief and depression since the time of Queen Victoria, so you do not have to suffer silently from depression like she did for more than half of her life.

With the proper outlets, treating grief-related depression can be very effective. Usually this means working through unfinished business and exploring the painful trauma associated with losing your loved one so that you can heal. Remember that your ultimate goal is to integrate your past and present feelings about your loved one so that you are able to reinvest your emotions into life and living and, ultimately, lift the cloud of sadness.

---

[1] Joseph Horatio Chant, "Queen Victoria," *Poetry Cat*, (Evesham, Worcestershire: Good, Stuff Ltd, 2016), http://www.poetrycat.com/joseph-horatio-chant/queen-victoria,.accessed September 21, 2016.

helplessness associated with having lost someone you love. There is often a sense of responsibility and a constant questioning why your loved one had to be the one who was ill, or if he or she has passed, the guilt might be related to why he or she died. This was true for Jack who questioned why he survived rather than his healthy older brother, a feeling with which Jack would struggle with quietly for the remainder of his life.

Joe Sr. and Rose's cultural and moral guilt

Daughter Rosemary Kennedy suffered from an undetermined mental disability. So little was known about the role genetics play in development in the early 1900s that the general idea was that abnormalities, or what we now know make each of us special, was some fault or sin of the parent or a that it was a punishment from God. The stigma and guilt her parents, Joe Sr. and Rose, experienced would have been grievous.

As Rosemary became a young woman, her awareness of the differences between her and her siblings grew, and so did her frustration. Her father, Joe, became increasingly concerned about her aggressive behaviors, which were mainly directed toward her mother. Joe Sr. secretly had a brain lobotomy performed on Rosemary. The neurosurgical procedure did not go well. Rosemary was never the same.

Joe Sr. and Rose had two distinctly different guilt responses to Rosemary's initial mental disability and subsequent life-changing procedure. Joe buried his cultural guilt regarding Rosemary, while Rose, who was devoutly Catholic, likely experienced moral guilt.

Cultural guilt is the inability to express what you or others may deem as the appropriate level of emotion and subsequently feel guilty about not being able to express that emotion. Each of us has personal and cultural expectations of how we think we should feel and behave in the face of loss. However, Joe would have had to bury much of his guilt and grief, because at the time, it was not culturally acceptable for men to express their feelings. The truth is that most of us have acted or failed to act and unintentionally hurt someone. It is just a part of life. Yet, when you do not address your cultural guilt, it can increase your burden and heavy your heart.

Moral guilt relates to feeling guilty about not being kind enough or about having had to say no, or perhaps you feel as though you did not spend enough time with your loved one, even though you have done all that you can. By all accounts, Rose had a deep devotion to God and family. However, one can assume that there were times when she felt uneasy about the fact that so much was out of her control when it came to her children. Because with moral guilt, there tends to be an evaluation of your own goodness, it seems that Rose was able to rely on her faith as a coping measure. Though, in some cases, *moral guilt* can act as an immobilizer of action because you simply do not know how to move forward. There are some specific suggestions for working through guilt in the chapter "Living without Guilt and Regret."

Bobby's recovery guilt

Bobby dedicated much of his life to protecting his older brother Jack. Yet his role of brother-protector extended far beyond their political oneness—Bobby was JFK's confidant, friend, and caregiver. When Jack died, Bobby experienced a guilt that he could not put behind him. Of course, there are always regrets when someone you love dies. Yet recovery guilt, frequently experienced during the first year following a death, is the feeling of guilt over wanting to get on with life following the loss. This type of guilt becomes a problem when it is a method of avoiding active participation in acts that make your life meaningful. Bobby experienced recovery guilt and likely for the rest of his life grieved the loss of Jack.

Working through guilt

Guilt is a complex emotion, however, the following are tips to begin coping with your feelings of guilt.

Forgiveness. Losing someone you love shakes up multiple relationships, including the relationship you have with yourself. Give yourself the gift of forgiveness and practice the art of self-preservation by appreciating your capabilities and what you have done to assist your loved one. Remember that whatever you did to care for or assist your loved one has been a display of your love and commitment.

Be self-supporting. Are you more self-critical than self-supporting? This can be difficult to assess accurately without professional assistance. However, most guilt does not stand up to reality testing. Remember, it is not the level of suffering that you experience as a result of your guilt that determines if your perceived debt has been paid. In fact, if you were to consider all that you have done to care for your loved one, you would come to the conclusion that you did the best you could and that you owe no debt. If you feel you need assistance to resolve guilt, do not be afraid to reach out and seek it.

Separate your view of yourself from the views of others. More often than not, guilt arises because you attach your personal views to another's view of who you are. Try not to fret about someone else's view of you and all that you did to care for your loved one, as this can impede your recovery.

You do not have to wait for others to acknowledge your level of commitment. Rather, give yourself permission to let go of the guilt, to make the best of your life, and to live each day with a dedication to fulfilling your purpose.

You have committed no offense in surviving. It is important to acknowledge that you have committed no offense by surviving. In fact, I would bet that more people than you know are happy that you are alive. Having cared for and about your loved one is a significant achievement, and making it through all you have is a testament to your strength.

As Edward Kennedy discussed in his tribute to his brother Bobby, reaching out attests to your ability to redirect guilt and grief so that you can make meaningful changes in your life and in the world.

It is important to recognize that you will likely not relieve your feelings associated with guilt all at once—it has taken time to develop your feelings; it will likely take time to let go of the guilt.

---

[1]Agamemnon of Aeschylus, BrainyQuote, (Xplore, Inc., 2016), http://www.brainyquote.com/quotes/quotes/a/aeschylus148591.html, accessed May 16, 2016.

The Transfer of Hope

Before you can live a part of you has to die. You have to let go of what could have been, how you should have acted and what you wish you would have said differently. You have to accept that you can't change the past experiences, opinions of others at that moment in time or outcomes from their choices or yours. When you finally recognize that truth then you will understand the true meaning of forgiveness of yourself and others. From this point you will finally be free.

– Shannon L. Alder[1]

In the movie *The Joy Luck Club*, the life imprints of three generations of Chinese American women are woven into a tapestry that speaks to the unbreakable bond that exists between mothers and daughters. The film's deeper meaning, however, centers on regret and the transfer of hope. This overarching theme is apparent in the loving but disconnected relationship between June (actress Ming-Na Wen) and her mother, Suyuan (actress Kieu Chinh), and expressed in a narrative about a beautiful swan.

Confounded by the story's meaning, June is not sure if the swan message is supposed to be a metaphor, but she continues to recite the narrative throughout the movie. When June's mother dies, her father (actor Chao Li Chi) seeks to comfort June in her grief by handing her an envelope that contains the swan feather. He explains that her mother waited for the day when she felt worthy enough to give the feather to June. Unfortunately Suyuan never did. June misses the chance to understand her mother, which becomes the source of her regret.

The Thin Line between Guilt and Regret

Regret is a uniquely human sentiment attributed to missed opportunities. In truth, if you never have any regrets, it may be an indication that you are disconnected from your feelings, as experiencing regret is often what prompts you to improve your circumstance.

The definitions for guilt and regret are often intermingled, and although they are closely related, there is a difference. Understanding the distinction between the two can be meaningful as you work to identify coping strategies.

Guilt, frequently experienced during the first year following a loss, is associated with the contradictory internal feelings resulting from thoughts about what could have or should have been done to support your loved one. Guilt may also include: the inability to express your emotions, a constant questioning about being healthy when your loved one was ill, and/or hesitancy in moving forward with your life after your loved one has passed. Positive guilt often leads to remorse, which is a healthy emotion and can be especially helpful when you know that you have treated someone unfairly. However, when you are grieving, most guilt does not stand up to reality testing. This means you more than likely did the best you could with what you knew at the time.

For example, I have not openly expressed feelings of guilt with regard to my Aunt Cynthia until now. Just before she passed away, it was determined that for her comfort and safety (she suffered from a bipolar disorder), it was in her best interest to move into a group home. This care situation didn't feel right, and I did not think that she would fare well. However, I convinced myself that I wasn't being rational.

When Aunt Cynthia passed away just two months later, I experienced a deep sense of guilt, which took a couple of years for me to resolve. My healing occurred when I was able to symbolically ask her for forgiveness and when I acknowledged the imprint that she left on my life.

On the other hand, not being able to say good-bye to my sister Rochelle has been a source of regret. She was in an abusive relationship and was injured to the point that she was unresponsive. I made plans to go to the hospital as soon as possible, but Rochelle lived about eighty miles away, and she passed away before I could get there. The distance kept me from being with her—it wasn't within my control—but I still regret not being able to physically say good-bye.

Avoiding the Dark Alley of Distress

Regret is not a dysfunctional or pathological condition that needs to be fixed. However, it can become a problem when it is used as a means of avoiding participation in acts that make your life meaningful. For example, should you find that you are mentally rehashing things that you said, you are playing back past actions, or you have a self-defeating attitude, it can lead to self-sabotage and a feeling of powerlessness.

Over time you may find that you are paralyzed from moving forward, and as a result, begin to experience distress, depression, or anxiety. The truth is that there is nothing healthy about dwelling on your regrets. Therefore, it is important to learn healthy ways to express your feelings so that you can avoid the dark alley of distress.

Transforming Your Regrets

Whenever possible, take the opportunity to transform your regrets by using your current insight to improve your actions in the future. Remember that it is what you learn that matters most. As was the case with June, every decision you have made may not have been an enlightened one. She was not aware of the tragic circumstances surrounding her mother's fleeing China during the Great War until her father shared the full story: that her mother had been married before, had borne twin daughters, and in her travels became violently ill.

Not wanting to die near her baby girls, Suyuan left them with everything she had under a giant tree in China, but woke up days later after being rescued. When she recovers, Suyuan relocates to the United States, without her twin daughters who remained lost in China, but she continued to write the Chinese authorities in search of them for the rest of her life.

Later, the twins are located and June takes a pilgrimage to meet them. In doing so, she fulfills her mother's long-cherished wish, to share the swan feather and the story that concludes, "this feather may look worthless but it comes from afar and brings with it all my good intentions."

The act of being able to do something for Suyuan empowers June to transform her regrets, and she inadvertently gains a better understanding of her mother.

Being empowered can be helpful as you to begin to accept that you can be a master of your own destiny moving forward. The following are three strategies that can be applied so that you are empowered to work through your feelings of regret:

Make sure that nothing goes unsaid. If there is something you need to say, make sure it does not go unsaid. If you love someone, tell this person; if you are happy, share your happiness; if you think that you hurt someone, take the time to make things right. If you find that you are continuing to rehash something that you did not have the opportunity to say to your loved one who has now passed, consider writing a private letter to express your feelings. Write down everything that you feel was left unsaid, and then read the letter out loud in private. You may choose to burn the letter, tear it up, or tie it to balloons and release it into the universe—do whatever you need to do to express your feelings and open the door for healing.

Nothing is permanent. No one will be here forever, not even you. It is important that you are not afraid to let go of the suffering of self-blame. Take time to appreciate everyone in the moment. In doing so, you are creating the possibility that your happiness will not depend on perfect conditions. In the Chinese culture, sky lanterns are said to have been used to communicate private messages. You may find it particularly therapeutic to integrate the release of sky lanterns as a part of a celebration of life service and attach both private messages to your loved one as well as your hopes for the future. Releasing sky lanterns is not only symbolic but an experience that you will not soon forget.

Don't be afraid to accept responsibility. Accept and determine how you can grow from each experience. Keep in mind that not every negative outcome is beyond your control. Therefore, it is important that you take responsibility, use your energy to create what can be, and do something different next time. Should you find that you are having trouble with replaying past words or actions in your head, consider making a worry box for your regrets. When the thought comes to mind, write it down and place it in the worry box. Give yourself a week or two, and then open the box. Completing this exercise may assist you in identifying common themes for your regret and lead to specific actions that you can take to make changes in the future.

Conventional wisdom says that you should live a life without regret, but perhaps the goal of life should not be to live a life without regret but to follow Henry David Thoreau's advice and "make the most of your regrets; never smother your sorrow, but tend and cherish it till it comes to have a separate and integral interest. Because to regret deeply is to live afresh."[3]

---

[1] Shannon Adler, Goodreads, (Goodreads, Inc., 2016). http://www.goodreads.com/author/show/1391130.Shannon_L_Alder, accessed May 16, 2016

[2] Amy Tan and Ronald Bass, *The Joy Luck Club*, directed by Wayne Wang (United States: Hollywood Pictures, 1993).

[3] Henry David Thoreau, BrainyQuote, (Xplore Inc., 2016), http://www.brainyquote.com/quotes/quotes/h/henrydavid133592.html, accessed May 16, 2016.

The Seven Spiritual Gs

Dandelion

*Like the dandelion,
so intoxicated with its own insignificance
in the greater scheme of things that it forgets
where it cannot grow, and it grows there anyway.*

—*Richard Schiffman*[1]

President Theodore (Teddy) Roosevelt was a man who led the country and his life with authority. Yet the popular images of the elder and more vigorous Theodore are in stark contrast to a man who was severely physically limited in his youth. In fact, he found his poor health and physical inabilities so frustrating that he dedicated his early years to overcoming them. Later, Theodore married a beautiful young lady named Alice and launched a successful political career. It seemed that nothing would stop Theodore from achieving any goal he set for himself.

Then, on Valentine's Day 1884, tragedy struck when his mother died in the early morning hours. That same day in the afternoon, Theodore's wife died as a result of an undiagnosed kidney disease—just two days after giving birth to their daughter.

Facing such tremendous grief, Theodore felt that the "light had gone out of his life."² So he packed up and headed to the wilderness of the Dakota Badlands, where he lived for the next three years.

Theodore's sojourn in the Badlands can be characterized as one of at least four pilgrimages that likely shaped his love of nature, strengthened his character, and awakened an inner strength that would be invaluable for the rest of his life. Tremendous insight about the resilience of the human spirit following the death of a loved one can be gleaned from his pilgrimages, and those of others, by using the seven Gs—grief, guilt, gossip, God, grace, goodness, and gifts—as the foundation for our discussion.

THREE PRECURSORS OF A PILGRIMAGE: GRIEF, GUILT, AND GOSSIP

Grief: The First Spiritual G

The Badlands served as a place of refuge and afforded Theodore the opportunity to work through his grief by becoming one with nature. You may also benefit from the opportunity to process your sadness by embarking on a pilgrimage. Although a spiritual pilgrimage usually relates to religious activities or rituals, it is often about strengthening what you believe. Therefore your pilgrimage might involve traveling to a place that you find religiously or spiritually significant, but it could also include saying a private prayer or spending time reading a poem or a book that brings you comfort.

What becomes most important is that you identify what it takes to nurture you spiritually, as it can be positive for coping, especially when your goal is to seek deeper meaning after loss. It is equally important to be mindful not to place time constraints on yourself. Just take into consideration the three years Theodore took to process his sadness and stay open to doing what you need to do to work through yours.

Gossip: The Second Spiritual G

In their grief, some individuals tend to gossip, and, rather than sharing their feelings with you, directly express their concerns, differences of opinions about care decisions, end-of-life choices, and even the funeral or memorial service arrangements with everyone except you.

Gossip under any circumstances can be harmful. Yet wagging tongues have a far greater impact when you are vulnerable and depending on your family, friends, and church for spiritual support.

Spiritual distress is not always the result of what people say but can relate to questions that you are not prepared to answer, that you find uncomfotable, or that remind you of your sadness. Just after my Aunt Cynthia's memorial service, the minister asked if she knew Christ before she died. It was such a dreadful question to ask at her service! Of course she did, but what if she had not; then what? With tears in our eyes and without saying a word, my cousin and I communicated, to one another, that if Aunt Cynthia had not made it to heaven, we didn't know who would.

Sometimes individuals you are depending on the most can unknowingly open you to greater hurt with words that are intended to provide comfort.

Feeling as though you are being talked about behind your back, that you are being judged, or that others are not sensitive to your feelings can result in a dramatic change in your social network, your church home, or your religous affiliation. As a result, you may end up modifying whom you spend time with or with whom you share your feelings and indirectly embark on a social pilgrimage.

Guilt: The Third Spiritual G

Bobby Kennedy's sense of guilt and resulting complicated spiritual distress were precursors to his pilgrimage. By pushing certain policies as attorney general, Bobby was convinced that he was responsible for his older brother JFK's assassination. Bobby questioned what he could have done to prevent such a tragedy and in turn needed time to reflect. He relied on his faith, silent reflection, and prayer to work through his sadness.

Yet his greatest comfort came from reading ancient Greek philosophy on grief and mortality. After all, who knew more about tragedy than the ancient Greeks?

This book features an entire chapter, *Living Without Fear or Regret*, dedicated to identifying and working through guilt. The key is first to recognize guilt for what it is and to acknowledge that it does not stand up to reality testing. Just as Bobby had to acknowledge that there was nothing he could have done to prevent his brother's passing, you, too, may have to accept that there is nothing you could have or should have done differently for your loved one.

WELCOMING GOD, GOODNESS, GIFTS, AND GRACE: THE RESULTS OF A ROAD WELL TRAVELED

God: The Fourth Spiritual G

Losing someone you love can alter how you feel about your connection with God. As a result, you may find that you are questioning your faith, that your faith is strengthened, or that your loss simply confirms what you believe.

As with any authentic and deeply private relationship, there may be times when you feel angry, frustrated, or scared. Or you have questions or experience an increased affinity to God or your Higher Being. But then He can handle your questions and frustration and accept your love. Therefore, it is paramount that you recognize that questioning does not mean that your faith is weak but that perhaps what you are feeling now will eventually bring you closer to God. This was true for my mother, but I leave it to you to determine your truth.

Grace: The Fifth Spiritual G

Grace following loss is often about knowing and then taking action when something is unhealthy for you spiritually. Although I am sure that Theodore was not thinking about grace but rather about self-preservation when he went on his pilgrimage, the act of removing himself from unhealthy situations by returning to the wilderness was grace in action.

In more passive terms, grace is free and undeserved, or divine assistance afforded by your higher power. It often serves as a buffer for grief because it is grace that provides you comfort in knowing that you will have the strength to eventually make it through your intense sadness. Taking time to work through your feelings takes grace, as does knowing when you have reached your limit and you no longer have to be strong for everyone else. Reaching out for support when it is needed and accepting assistance are also acts of displaying grace, even if you do not recognize this at the time.

Gifts: The Sixth Spiritual G

One of the best speeches ever given was orated by Bobby Kennedy, just moments after Martin Luther King Jr. was assassinated. Bobby was a naturally gifted speaker, yet I wonder, if he had not experienced such tremendous grief and diligently studied ancient Greek writings, would he have given such an impassioned speech? The words he spoke on that night in 1968 saved an entire city.

Grief can propel you to identify your spiritual gifts. Generally described as natural talents or areas where you excel, spiritual gifts have common themes and are things that you have loved to do throughout your life. Writing has always been my passion, yet some of my most introspective writing came after my grandmother died. She was the inspiration for my second book *At the Heart of the Matter: A Spiritual Journey for Caregivers*. You might say that my grief helped me find my voice.

You have gifts that you can share, even if you are unable to identify them right now. Getting in tune with your spiritual gifts can be helpful in deciding what you will do next. Therefore, it is vital that you acknowledge what you do well, take care to develop your gifts, and recognize their value as a necessary component of your healing.

Goodness: The Seventh Spiritual G

Theodore Roosevelt National Park is one of five parks and hundreds of conservation efforts that represent Teddy's committment to giving something back. From the time of his youth, Teddy leaned on his passion for nature as encouragement for overcoming his physical limitations, as an outlet for his grief, and as a refuge whenever he needed to recalibrate. Knowing that everyone should have the opportunity to benefit from communing with nature, Teddy ensured that these natural resources were preserved for generations to come. His work to preserve nature is a testament to his goodness.

How you share your insight is a contributing factor to a well-rounded pilgrimage. It also might be an approach toward acknowledging your loss and processing your grief in a way that adds meaning to your life and the lives of others; in fact, your sharing is a display of your goodness.

Although it is common to experience sadness when you are grieving, even when you are sad, you retain the ability to feel pleasant emotions. Generally you hold on to the ability to find meaning in your life and, over time, establish a new equilibrium so that you can resume normal activity. It is hoped that by gaining a clearer understanding of the seven Gs' and how they can impact you emotionally, you will be empowered to embrace your spiritual pilgrimage to work through your sorrow.

You may be experiencing complicated spiritual grief if: your sadness lasts six months or longer with a general disengagement from participation in normal, everyday life activities; you bury your feelings; or that you overall feel hopeless. Complicated spiritual grief is usually precipitated by the loss of someone who is significant in your life, or a quest for deeper understanding about the meaning and purpose of life, and results in answers to your questions that are unsettling, nonsensical, or both.

Although not all loss leads to spiritual questioning, it is common to experience *complicated spiritual grief* if you have cared for a loved one with a debilitating or terminal illness, if your loved one experienced a great deal of pain, or if you have unresolved feelings associated with your loss.

Seeking professional counseling and care is essential to working through complicated spiritual grief. Venting is critical, as is finding someone who is a good listener and who will allow you to share your feelings without repercussions. The goal is working through any unfinished business associated with your spiritual distress so that you achieve spiritual wellness.

---

[1] Schiffman, By Richard. "Clever Stalk.", Poem.. http://www.best-poems.net/richard_schiffman/clever_stalk.html, accessed on. May 15, 2016.

[2] Theodore Roosevelt, "The life has gone out of my life," Ford Library Museum, https://www.fordlibrarymuseum.gov/museum/exhibits/TR/light.htm.,accessed on May 14, 2016

Part Two: Reflections For Your Soul

Close your eyes and open the windows of your heart to reflection and introspection as it is the first step to healing your soul.

—Dr. Eboni Green

Four Questions to Frame Your Pilgrimage

To grieve is to know you are alive. Through tears sorrow is expressed and loss is heartfelt.
To grieve is to recognize a purposeful life. Gloomy days when you are not able to get out of
bed—those days occur for the grieving soul impacted by a loss. Mourning through tears, sometimes laughing or smiling at a special memory, confirms that you are still alive. Years may pass, and sometime those years are many, but the memories never go away. Grief may change its form to stories about our lost loves, remembrances of the playful years.
Yet, if you sit silently for just a moment, sometimes you can feel the sweet kisses and whispers of love carried in the wind. Yes, I would have to say, grieving lets you know you are still alive.

—Dr. Eboni Ivory Green

Being blessed with life almost certainly guarantees that you will experience the pain of losing someone you love. Being a caregiver often increases the likelihood that you will experience feelings of loss both while your loved one is living and long after he or she has gone. I know that this was true for my mother when she took care of my aunt Linda following her diagnosis with terminal ovarian cancer. In fact, Aunt Linda's passing was the first of many losses my mother experienced that left her emotionally fragile.

Like many grieving caregivers, she stopped trusting her instincts. After years of leading a successful life and having a stellar career as a lawyer, her sense of security was disrupted, she questioned her spiritual beliefs. As a result, my mother's identity radically shifted. She wasn't able to talk to anyone about her despair because she hurt so deeply and she buried her sorrow. Most people in her inner circle thought she was uncharacteristically resilient, and others were wondering how she'd made it through all that she had. But the truth was that she was falling apart. In no uncertain terms, she was shattered.

Leon Weistler shares that "there are circumstances that must shatter you; and if you are not shattered, then you have not understood your circumstances. In such circumstances, it is a failure for your heart not to break, and it is pointless to put up a fight, for a fight will blind you to the opportunity that has been presented by your misfortune."[1]

Indeed it was only when my mother began to recognize her internal turmoil by facing her feelings head-on that she was able to start to process her sadness. In time she was able to acknowledge that she was in fact on a pilgrimage of grief. Then she was able to actively seek healing by dedicating herself to personal transformation. For a time, achieving self-actualization became the most important thing in her life. She ultimately began to trust her own instincts, reactions, and abilities by looking inward.

Four questions for documenting your pilgrimage

So how do you begin to move forward when you have been shattered by grief? It will likely not be easy. In fact, it will take time to process all that you have been through. Yet, you are invited to ponder four very important questions that may help organize your thoughts as you document your pilgrimage and begin to process your sadness.

Question 1

What are you being pulled from? During a lecture about the pilgrimage of aging, Jane M. Thibault shared food for thought when she said, "The old life was a good life but it is no longer available to you. It has been carried away irreversibly."[2] Loss changes your life, but what is most important now is that you take this opportunity to truly evaluate where you have been focusing your energy and make adjustment if needed so that you are dedicated to doing something meaningful in your life moving forward.

Question 2

What has been the most constant aspect of your life? Is there something that you are being compelled to learn about yourself? By identifying aspects of your life that have remained constant, themes may emerge. There may be people whom you love and whom you might also lean upon and places or things that bring you comfort to aid in your healing. If there ever was a time to pinpoint what is important in your life, the time is now.

Question 3

What are you being nudged or invited to do? I recently interviewed Linda Losey, who lost two sons in a short period of time. On June 22, 2004, her youngest son, Sam, was crushed beneath the wheels of a trailer hauling a five-ton tractor; he did not survive and was only ten years old. Just when she was beginning to make peace with losing Sam, her intense spiritual grief was complicated when her eighteen-year-old son Eric, a U.S. Marine, took his own life. Her pilgrimage started with keeping a promise which was to someday horseback across the country with her younger son Sam. Having lost Sam, Linda traveled 4,032 miles across the country on horseback alone.

When Linda's eighteen-year-old son died tragically just a little over a year after her cross-country trip, she was shattered. It took time for her to find meaning in life again, but she opened an award-winning distillery, which she describes as the happiest place on earth. You may have to dig deep, but I would bet there is something that you are being nudged or invited to do.

Question 4

How you will share what you have learned? For my mom, her greatest steps toward healing were accomplished when she began to actively share what she was learning on her pilgrimage. When she read something that spoke to her, she would share it; if she meditated, prayed, or reflected and gained clarity, she made sure to share that too.

Is there a book that you might write or a conference where you might present, a friend who could benefit from your knowledge? Do whatever you can to share, share, and share.

Reflections for the Soul was written to speak directly to you if you have cared for and lost someone you love. Just as your feelings are often dictated by your experiences, your support system, and your ability to be resilient, working through grief is dependent on a variety of factors, including your willingness to (1) acknowledge your feelings, (2) stay open to being inspired, and (3) reflect deeply. All three are important for your growth.

Stay open to being Inspired. Orignial poems, inspirational stories, and famous quotes are provided to move you into deeper levels of reflection through your pilgrimage of self-care and healing.

Acknowledge your feelings and Reflect Deeply. You will be prompted to (1) acknowledge your feelings; (2) let go of unhealthy emotions, practices, and people; (3) commit to introspection; and (4) actively seek opportunities for transformation.

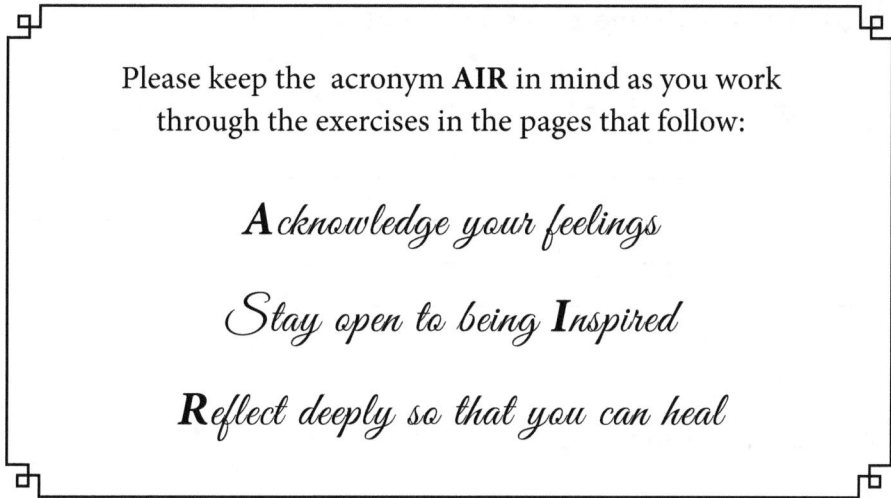

Please keep the acronym **AIR** in mind as you work through the exercises in the pages that follow:

Acknowledge your feelings

Stay open to being Inspired

Reflect deeply so that you can heal

Whether you decide to take a physical trek to a place that you find meaningful or determine that your sojourn will occur within, what matters most is that you have the opportunity for significant reflection, for meaningful introspection, and that you take the opportunity to commune by sharing the insights you glean from your journey.

Acknowledge your feelings

What are you being pulled from?

_____
_____
_____
_____
_____

What has been the most constant aspect of your life?

_____
_____
_____
_____
_____

What are you being nudged or invited to do?

_____
_____
_____
_____
_____

How will you share your pilgrimage?

_____
_____
_____
_____
_____

Stay open to being Inspired

I don't know who I am. And I don't think people ever will know who they are. We have to be humble enough to learn to live with this mysterious question. Who am I? So, I am a mystery to myself. I am someone who is in this pilgrimage from the moment that I was born to the day to come that I'm going to die. And this is something that I can't avoid, whether I like it or not, or—I'm going to die. So, what I have to do is to honor this pilgrimage through life. And so I am this pilgrim—if I can somehow answer your question—who's constantly amazed by this journey. Who is learning a new thing every single day? But who's not accumulating knowledge, because then it becomes a very heavy burden on your back. I am this person who is proud to be a pilgrim, and who's trying to honor his journey.

—Paulo Coehlo[3]

Reflect deeply so that you can heal

Close your eyes for just a moment, if you will, and imagine that you are traveling to a place of spiritual or religious significance that is tucked away in a remote region thousands of miles away. The voyage is arduous, but when you finally arrive at your destination, the scenery is more magnificent than you visualized, your soul vibrates, and you are revitalized. You take the opportunity to acknowledge that having made it to such a divine location is a testament to your inner strength. You are refreshed! Now open your eyes. You have just taken a mental pilgrimage.

---

[1] Shared in Mark Nepos's book *Finding Inner Courage*, pg. 133.

[2] Jane M. Thibault, "Pilgrimage: A Way of Being on the Aging Journey," presented at the sixth International Conference on Aging and Spirituality, Los Angeles, CA, 2015, http://www.6thinternationalconference.org/#!presentations-handouts-downloads/c1rdu, accessed June 2, 2016.

[3] P. Coehlo, "Quotes about Pilgrimage," 2016, http://www.goodreads.com/quotes/tag/pilgrimage, accessed June 2, 2016.

Take a Whack at Ouiser

The dust devil has its genesis when a few loose particles of dirt come together and catch in the wind. Leaping, vibrating, and then collecting, until it becomes a violent storm. The black blizzard disrupts your air quality so that you cannot breathe and clouds your vision so that you are unable to see what is in front of you. It destroys everything in its wake. Then, after a time, the harmattan simply loses steam and suddenly dissipates, just like anger.

—Dr. Eboni Green

In 1985, Robert Harling[1] penned a theatrical work that was based on the true story of his sister's lifelong struggle with diabetes. Later, his play would become the widely successful movie *Steel Magnolias*, staring actress Sally Field as his mother (M'Lynn) and Julia Roberts as his sister (Shelby). In what is arguably one of the most realistic portraits of a grieving mother, M'Lynn lifts the veil of anger following the death of her only daughter when she says:

> *I want to know why Shelby's life is over! I wanna know how that baby will ever know how wonderful his mother was! Will he ever know what she went through for him! Oh, God, I wanna know why? Why? Lord, I wish I could understand! I, I don't think I can take this! I, I just wanna hit somebody 'til they feel as bad as I do! I just wanna hit something! I wanna hit it hard!*

Just as it appears as though she will be consumed by her anger and runs the risk of becoming unhinged, a lifelong friend, Clairee (Olympia Dukakis), suggests that M'Lynn take a whack at their ornery neighbor Ouiser (Shirley MacLaine). Initially, M'Lynn is confounded to the point that she pauses her impassioned plea and stares blankly at Clairee and Ouiser. Her friend's absurd suggestion not only serves as a welcomed distraction but lightens the mood as well. The women are unable to contain their dismay and erupt into laughter when Clairee says, "M'Lynn, you just missed the chance of a lifetime! Half o' Chinquapin Parish'd give their eye teeth to take a whack at Ouiser!"

M'Lynn's emotional honesty serves as confirmation that anger is an appropriate and prudent response to losing someone you love and that expressing your frustration is equally fitting. Even though you may be uncomfortable expressing your feelings, it is important to remember that the discomfort you may experience now is not the greatest risk to your healing. Rather, the greatest risk to your emotional well-being lies in suppressing your feelings. The following are two misconceptions and three common truths about grief and anger.

TWO COMMON MISCONCEPTIONS ABOUT ANGER

Misconception 1: Good people do not suffer.

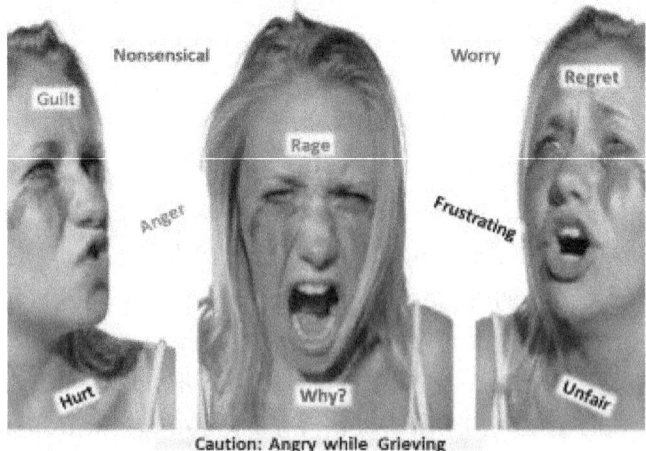

Caution: Angry while Grieving

The truth is that even if you live your life with integrity, you will likely witness and experience both physical and emotional pain. Having to bear witness to suffering is not only distressing but also can also be a major source of anger, especially when you love someone and his or her discomfort appears to be endless or nonsensical.

The miniseries *Deadwood*[2] provides an excellent example of senseless suffering and emotional exacerbation when Doc Cochran (actor Brad Dourif) reaches his breaking point while caring for Reverend Smith (actor Ray McKinnon), who is enduring relentless and debilitating seizures that render him blind and immobile.

Having to care for a good man in such agony leaves Doc Cochran vexed and crying aloud for God to intervene. Although the story is fictional, the emotion is real and closely aligns with how you may feel after having cared for a good person who did not deserve to suffer. You will likely not make sense of the suffering, but the road to gaining strength involves acknowledging and accepting your anger and then expressing exactly how you feel in the moment.

Misconception 2: It is improper to express your anger.

Are you unable to express your anger, so that rather than stating your frustrations in a constructive manner, you display an uncomfortable grin, laugh inappropriately, or detach so that you do not have to acknowledge your feelings? If the answer is yes, perhaps you are like many who were taught that it is improper to express your anger, when the truth is that anger is an appropriate response to some situations.

In fact, if you look to M'Lynn as an example, you know that expressing anger and sadness is both healthy and necessary. What turns out to be unhealthy is suppressing your feelings, holding in your rage, and/or turning your feelings inward, as behaviors such as excessive drinking, smoking, and overeating are often the end result. Instead, make every effort to address what is making you angry, express how you are feeling in a constructive manner, and, when possible, move on.

THREE COMMON TRUTHS ABOUT RELEASING ANGER

It is important to take time to process your feelings.

Are you angry right now? If so, it is probably not the right time to have a heart-to-heart conversation about your feelings of grief, your aggravations about care decisions that were made for your loved one, or any other unresolved matters. Why? Because in your frustration, it is easy to say things that you do not really mean or that can be particularly hurtful.

What works best is taking time to process your feelings prior to sharing your thoughts. For example, you might count to ten, go for a walk, or simply remove yourself from a situation that is causing you to be upset so that you have the opportunity to process your feelings. When you are calm enough to express yourself, it is important to remember that what you say should not be accusatory and should be free from defensive comments. Each of the aforementioned tips has been found to be counterproductive but is among natural communication responses when you are angry. I encourage you to take the time you need to process your thoughts so that when you decide to communicate your feelings, you have your emotions in check.

It is healthy to release negative energy.

Negative energy can build up just like steam in a boiling teapot, and it has to be released; otherwise, it will spill over into other areas of your life. For example, if you are not addressing your feelings, you might be cross or short with people in your inner circle, and as a result, you may find that you are alienated because others do not know how to respond to your anger.

Suppressed negative energy can also result in a predisposition to colds, depression, and other ailments. The truth is that, as hard as you try, you are not protecting anyone by hiding your feelings. One of the best ways to release negative energy is to participate in regular physical activity.

However, with grief, there may simply be things that have gone unsaid that need to be expressed, and there are likely other feelings hidden beneath your anger that must be addressed. Writing an open letter and reading it out loud and in its entirety, without interruption, can work to diffuse your anger. You may choose to read it alone or with someone you trust and then discard the document as a symbolic way of letting go of the negative energy.

Distancing yourself from people and situations that make you angry is a form of self-preservation.

Grief and anger are complex emotions. You may find that you are quite changed by your grief, and as a result, you may find that you have outgrown certain relationships. This may mean that you no longer spend your time doing things that you used to find enjoyable. You may also determine that being around certain people or being placed in a specific situation consistently causes you to feel angry. It might be a good time to create space, even if just for a period of time.

Taking a break from people or situations that frustrate you can help you defuse your anger, and it may also help you preserve those relationships, so that later down the road, should you feel differently, you will not have burned any bridges or ruined relationships.

When you are grieving, you may find that your feelings of anger are intensified. What is most important is that you identify what is making you angry and then work toward releasing and resolving those emotions in a healthy and constructive manner.

Acknowledge your feelings

What are three strategies or approaches you can use to let off steam when you are angry?

_____
_____
_____
_____

Do you have a hard time saying the phrase "I am angry" or "I feel angry"? Please explain.

_____
_____
_____
_____

Is there someone you feel has violated you in some way that causes you to feel angry? What steps of forgiveness need to be taken to bring closure to the situation?

_____
_____
_____
_____

Stay open to being Inspired

Learn this from me. Holding anger is a poison. It eats you from inside. We think that hating is a weapon that attacks the person who harmed us. But hatred is a curved blade. And the harm we do, we do to ourselves.

—Mitch Albom[3]

Reflect deeply so that you can heal

Time spent with caregiving has placed demands on your time, energy, money, and taken priority. You may look in the mirror and not even remotely know who you are outside of your role as a caregiver. You may have been so entrenched in resolving your loved one's circumstances and in turn not have had the opportunity to fully express your sadness and anger.

But it is healthy to vent about resentments that may have resulted from providing care. Anger as an emotion can be a tool to propel you to action. It is up you to recognize, acknowledge, and work toward releasing your anger.

---

[1] Robert Harling, *Steel Magnolias*, directed by Herbert Ross (United States: Tristar Pictures, 1989). Quotation from http://www.imdb.com/title/tt0098384/?ref_=ttco_co_tt, accessed September 21, 2016.

[2] David Miltch, *Deadwood*, performed by Brad Dourif, Ray McKinnon (United States: CBS Paramount Network Television, 2004), DVD.

[3] Mitch Albom, Good Reads.com, http://www.goodreads.com/quotes/141065-learn-this-from-me-holding-anger-is-a-poison-it, accessed on September 30, 2016.

Cultivating Life-Enhancing Spirituality

No one can take away the memories of who we were together. All that we shared with one another, the hearty laughs, the doleful tears we shed, the times when we sat peacefully and didn't need to say a word; the memory of you and all that we mean to one another will never fade.
—Dr. Eboni Green

In the book *Moments of Guidance in the Presence of God*, David Jeremiah tells a story about a six-hundred-year-old Norwegian spruce tree. The tree is said to be the oldest living plant on earth with roots that are believed to predate Bible patriarch Abraham.

Jeremiah writes that "whenever a stem or trunk dies, a new one emerges from the root stock,"[1] so that the tree is constantly growing. To me, the story of the spruce tree suggests that there is a possibility for spiritual growth after loss.

The psychological strain of loss can result in a questioning or a confirmation of your faith. For my husband, Terrence, cultivating his spiritual well-being was a natural and necessary response to losing both his stepfather and dad within a short period of time. His emotional devastation coupled with the responsibility of having to hold two families together left him spiritually depleted.

In fact, losing Johnny and Odell felt as though two majestic oak trees had gone missing from the forest, and although it has taken time for him to process the deep feelings of sadness, Terrence's ability to recognize that their massive roots will continue to spout new stems has provided him a small measure of comfort. Hermann Hesse offers further reassurance regarding losing such distinguished men:

> *For me, trees have always been the most penetrating preachers. I revere them when they live in tribes and families, in forests and groves. And even more I revere them when they stand alone. They are like lonely persons. Not like hermits who have stolen away out of some weakness, but like great, solitary men, like Beethoven and Nietzsche.*
>
> *In their highest boughs the world rustles, their roots rest in infinity; but they do not lose themselves there, they struggle with all the force of their lives for one thing only: to fulfill themselves according to their own laws, to build up their own form, to represent themselves. Nothing is holier, nothing is more exemplary than a beautiful, strong tree.*
>
> *When a tree is cut down and reveals its naked death-wound to the sun, one can read its whole history in the luminous, inscribed disk of its trunk: in the rings of its years, its scars, all the struggle, all the suffering, all the sickness, all the happiness and prosperity stand truly written, the narrow years and the luxurious years, the attacks withstood, the storms endured.*
>
> *And every young farm boy knows that the hardest and noblest wood has the narrowest rings, that high on the mountains and in continuing danger the most indestructible, the strongest, the ideal trees grow.*[2]

After reading Hess' words, will you ever look at a tree in the same way again? I know that I will not. Yet I would be remiss if I did not share that, just as the earth is forever changed by the death of a life-giving tree, so too will your spiritual landscape likely be changed as a result of losing someone you love. In reality, the strain of loss often leads to a strengthening of your faith or results in a questioning of your faith. Or your loss may simply confirm what you believe.

Loss confirming what you believe

When my grandmother died, the grief I experienced was unbearable. Yet beneath the pain I found spiritual comfort in her peaceful homegoing. For me, the way she lived her life highlighted the importance of **striving to live in a manner that is consistent with your core values** and confirmed that, in doing so, you are not only nurturing your inner **being** but also freeing your soul to focus on your life's purpose.

For example, if you are compassionate, driven, or loyal, living, affirming, and embracing your truth increases the likelihood that you will experience some measure of peace. Knowing these truths gave me solace, and I hope that you too are comforted. As a matter of fact, the timing could not be better for you to begin nurturing what is the most important part of your being by incorporating your core values and the art of BEING into your daily life.

I freely admit that it took time to open my eyes to the importance of **BEING**. The truth is that I almost worked myself to death—*literally*—before I got the message! My problem was that I wasn't focusing on living in a manner that was consistent with nurturing my core... simply put, I was doing too much!

Are you doing too much or always focusing on the needs of others? Or are you taking time to nurture your BEING? One way to test whether you are in tune with your spiritual core is to answer an important question: are you taking time simply to **BE,** *or do you feel that you must be* **DOING** *something all the time?* If you were to carefully peel away the layers of your personhood, what would remain is your spiritual core *or you're* **BEING**; it is the essence of who you are and what makes you-unique, and it must be nurtured! Should you find that you spend the majority of your time focused on external issues or feel that you always need to be doing something, you are likely missing out on a very important aspect of life. Namely, getting to know what is most important to you, shaping your legacy, and nurturing your spirutal **BEING.**

My grandmother's passing confirmed my spiritual beliefs by forcing me to reevaluate what was most important in my life, and as a result, I began to focus my energy inward.

Loss as a precursor to strengthened faith

The loss of a loved one can be a precursor to strengthened faith. This was true for my husband, Terrence, when his stepfather, Johnny, died in 2014 after a long battle with lung cancer. Then, just as Terrence began facing his sadness, his dad Odell received a terminal diagnosis and passed away. Only after Terrence reflected on the life imprints of

Johnny and Odell could he identify activities that would enhance his spiritual well-being.

Johnny taught Terrence to be straightforward, to care for his family, and to become one with nature. Terrence gleaned from his dad how to live off the land, how to be a strategic thinker, and how to regard measured action. Once Terrence had the opportunity to acknowledge all that his stepfather and dad modeled to him—he started to experience emotional relief.

But, deeper healing only occurred as a result of Terrence's **ACTIVE** involvement in seeking out opportunities to enhance his *spiritual well-being*. For him, fishing, hunting, and embracing his love of nature were the most important components of strengthening his faith.

In retrospect, I am thankful for the contributions Johnny and Odell made to my husband's life and upbringing, for the richness they added to our lives, and for the love they showered upon our children.

Most important, I am grateful for their collective teachings, which have afforded Terrence the opportunity to achieve spiritual wellness and self-actualization because they gave him roots by teaching him to love nature.

Spiritual wellness is usually achieved through a combination of activities. Generally speaking, activities that are spiritually enhancing have common themes and are the things that you have loved to do for a lifetime. I would suggest that spiritual wellness is a marriage of the mind, body, and spirit that often incorporates faith, belief, religion, and self-actualization.

The path to spiritual wellness may involve meditation, prayer, affirmations, or specific spiritual practices that support your connection to your higher power or belief system. Stillness, yoga, and meditation can also help you achieve spiritual wellness.

What is most important is that you identify what it takes to nurture your spirituality, as it can be positive for coping, especially when your goal is to seek deeper meaning after loss. It is vital that you be diligent in finding strategies to nurture yourself. Remember that the goal is to actively engage in activities that contribute to your spiritual growth.

Loss: Has your faith been shaken?

Complicated spiritual grief is usually precipitated by the loss of someone who is significant in your life, or a quest for deeper understanding about the meaning and purpose of life, and results in answers to your questions that are unsettling, nonsensical, or both. Although not all loss leads to spiritual questioning, it is common to experience *complicated spiritual grief* if you have cared for a loved one with a debilitating or terminal illness or if your loved one experienced a great deal of pain. Spiritual grief can also occur if you have unresolved feelings associated with your loss. Should you find that you are experiencing spiritual distress or complicated spiritual grief, I hope that you take comfort in knowing that you are not alone and that questioning does not mean that your faith is weak but that perhaps what you are feeling now will eventually bring you closer to God.

Experiencing spiritual distress can be scary, so much so that you should not try to go it alone. Instead, reach out to someone whom you trust so that you can talk to him or her about how you are feeling. If your distress is not alleviated, it might be time to seek help from a professional counselor or therapist.

Try to be mindful not to place time constraints on yourself. It is your soul that determines your divine pace. Remember that you are mapping your appropriate healing and that you can facilitate this by welcoming the epiphany, awaking, as it occurs through your dedication to care for you.

Acknowledge your feelings

Are you living in a manner that is consistent with your core? If the answer is yes, please move to the next question. If the answer is no, what might you do to make sure that you are living in a manner that is consistent with your inner core?

_____
_____
_____
_____
_____

Take a moment to reflect upon and then define your life's purpose? Is there anything that inhibits you from living your life's purpose? If so, is there anything you can do to actively eliminate the barrier?

_____
_____
_____
_____
_____

How will you incorporate simply **BEING** into your daily life?

_____
_____
_____
_____
_____

Stay open to being Inspired

In oneself lies the whole world and if you know how to look and learn, the door is there and the key is in your hand. Nobody on earth can give you either the key or the door to open, except yourself.

—Jiddu Krishnamurti[2]

Reflect deeply so that you can heal

When we are stricken and cannot bear our lives any longer, then a tree has something to say to us: Be still! Be still! Look at me! Life is not easy, life is not difficult. Those are childish thoughts. Let God speak within you, and your thoughts will grow silent. You are anxious because your path leads away from mother and home.
But every step and every day lead you back again to the mother. Home is neither here nor there. Home is within you, or home is nowhere at all.

—Hermann Hesse[3]

---

[1] David Jeremiah, *Moments of Guidance in the Presence of God* (New York: Hachette, 2011), page 5.

[2] Jiddu Krishnamurti, BrainyQuote, (Xplore, Inc., 2016), http://www.brainyquote.com/quotes/authors/j/jiddu_krishnamurti.html, accessed September 30, 2016.

[3] Hermann Hesse, *Bäume. Betrachtungen und Gedichte* (Germany: Insel, 1984), http://www.goodreads.com/book/show/1552368.B_ume_Betrachtungen_und_Gedichte, accessed September 21, 2016.

The Grace to Grieve

I am waiting purposefully because anything long lasting requires patience. I am waiting patiently and purposefully for clarity. Yes, I am waiting, as I know that all will be revealed in good time.

—Dr. Eboni Ivory Green

Growing up, I confided in my grandmother a great deal. Not only was she an attentive listener but also she was also very wise. When I became an adult, the focus of our conversations undoubtedly transitioned so that I would confide in her whenever I was making a major life decision. Most of the time, she did not give direct advice, but when she did, one theme emerged, which was to *give it a year*!

What my grandmother was actually saying is that when something major occurs in your life, it is prudent to take time to process your thoughts and feelings. For her, a year was measurable, and for me, it was a time frame that was easy to wrap my brain around. In time, I came to understand the phrase *give it a year* as metaphor for patience.

Patience is a necessity when you are grieving, as you will need time to process your feelings. When you think about having patience, it is often related to external experiences, yet internal patience is what is needed most when you are heartbroken.

I invite you to take the *Collins English Dictionary* definition of patience, which is a "quiet, steady perseverance, diligent, and even-tempered care,"[2] and focus these words internally to enhance your emotional intelligence as you work through your sorrow.

FOUR POWERFUL WAYS TO PRACTICE PATIENCE AS YOU GRIEVE

To get you started, here are four powerful ways you can practice internal patience in your grief.

The grace to grieve.

It will take time to work through your feelings, and as a result, you will likely need to be patient. The last thing you want to end up doing is stretching yourself too thin or placing pressure on yourself to get over your feelings. It is equally important to acknowledge when you have reached your limit and you no longer have to be strong for anyone else, you do not have to follow someone else's road map for grief.

For some time, you may feel as though you are falling apart, and that is also okay. What matters most is that you accept the grace to grieve and have comfort in knowing that you will make it through your intense sadness, in your own time and in your own way.

Being self-aware.

Building self-trust is what matters most right now. If you are running on empty, you will be prone to growing impatient even when it comes to yourself. Building self-trust and being self-aware of your feelings will give you a chance to reconstruct an environment that is conducive to your healing. In essence, you are taking this opportunity to identify what is healthy for you now and what may benefit you in the future.

Put things into perspective.

Take a step back and remove yourself from the opinions of others so you can determine what you need to do in your life to heal. A couple of months ago, my niece Alisha received a message from someone whom she considered a close friend that was telling her she should just get over her grief. It has been a little over a year since her mother, who was also my sister, died under tragic circumstances, and Alisha was shattered by these comments.

We had to remind Alisha that what she is doing is keeping the memory of her mother alive in a way that is both healthy and meaningful. The comments were unfortunate, however, the conversation we had as a family helped Alisha understand that she must continue to be patient with her grief and that her journey is personal.

Remember it is the journey.

As David Bednar stated, "sometimes we may ask God for success, and He gives us physical and mental stamina. We might plead for prosperity, and we receive enlarged perspective and increased patience, or we petition for growth and are blessed with the gift of grace. He may bestow upon us conviction and confidence as we strive to achieve worthy goals."[3]

You will likely gradually develop the strength to remain patient even in the most trying situations if you are able to keep in mind that you are on a journey to healing. Have patience and be strong!

You will likely face many difficulties as you try to carve out what is normal for you now. It is important to take the time needed to adjust to your loss. In fact, I would suggest that it is simply okay to go with the flow for a while; try not to place any extra pressure on yourself by making any immediate, major changes in your life. Typically, your next steps will reveal themselves in good time.

A cknowledge you feelings

How can you use what you are learning to help you move forward?

_____
_____
_____

What steps might you take so that you can get back to feeling comfortable, safe, and productive?

_____
_____
_____

On a scale of 1 to 10 (with 1 being the lowest), please rate your overall sense of patience today, then explain why you chose this number.

_____
_____
_____

How might increasing your patience contribute to your healing?

_____
_____
_____

Stay open to being Inspired

I beg you, to have patience with everything unresolved in your heart and to try to love the questions themselves as if they were locked rooms or books written in a very foreign language. Don't search for the answers, which could not be given to you now, because you would not be able to live them. And the point is to live everything. Live the questions now. Perhaps then, someday far in the future, you will gradually, without even noticing it, live your way into the answer.

–Rainer Maria Rilke, Letters to a Young Poet[4]

Reflect deeply so that you can heal

Sometimes patience and stillness are gained by doing things that revitalize you, for example, having the grace to get to know yourself and fortitude to take time to gain a better understanding of what is going to make you happy. It is OK to be selfish for a while. I hope that you will give yourself the gift of time. Being patient with yourself while you grieve is a vital component to self-care and healing.

---

[1] Auliq Ice. Good Reads.com http://www.goodreads.com/author/show/11353736.Auliq_Ice, accessed September 30, 2016.

[2] *Collins English Dictionary Online,* s.v. "patience," http://dictionary.reference.com/browse/patience, accessed September 30, 2016.

[3] David A. Bednar. BrainyQuote.com, Xplore Inc, 2016. https://www.brainyquote.com/quotes/authors/d/david_a_bednar.html, accessed September 30, 2016.

[4] Rainer Marie Rilke. Good Reads.com http://www.goodreads.com/quotes/563483-i-beg-you-to-have-patience-with-everything-unresolved-in, accessed September 30, 2016.

Living Without Guilt or Regret?

Today I start anew. I clear the slate of yesterday's woes and in doing so open my heart and soul to the newness of the day. The new day starts with boldness like no other, and as I visualize how this new day will start, I encounter feelings of excitement I never thought possible. The day reminds me that the sun can and always does rise again so that I can begin anew. As I ponder this new beginning, I give myself authority to experience a wide range of emotions. For it is through these feelings that my identity is formed. I am reminded that the mountains, however still and mighty, are not fully appreciated until one has seen the glowing sun shine brightly on the mountain's peak. Yesterday's regrets are in the past. Today I will focus on the opportunity that exists, because it is a new day, and with each new day, I have the chance to begin afresh.

—Dr. Eboni Green

Rose Fitzgerald Kennedy's life can be compared, both in opulence and tragedy, to that of ancient Greek nobility. For a fleeting moment in time, her family was viewed as royalty, an idea that originated with her daughter-in-law Jackie O's evoking the myth of Camelot when Rose's son Jack became the first Irish Catholic president in American history. At the same time John was elected president, Bobby became attorney general; Rose was confirmed as papal countess for her many charitable works, and later the family founded the Special Olympics (in honor of Rosemary).

Yet no matter how hard she strived, Rose faced tremendous grief. In fact, Barbara Gibson said the following of Mrs. Kennedy: "Her maternal sensitivity to the slightest hint that her children had turned out anything but perfect made me understand why the thought of Rosemary still caused her such torment."[1] Rose's sadness further deepened when, within a short period of time, she lost four of her children and then her husband suffered from a debilitating stroke that left him devoid of speech. When asked about her life, Rose reflected:

> *In my life, I am often reminded that there is a destiny that rules over us, because no one whom I know about or whom I read about seems to be completely happy during a long time. Our family was the perfect family—boys brilliant, girls attractive and intelligent, money, prestige, a young father and mother of intelligence, devoted, exemplary habits and successful in the education of the children.*
>
> *Joe Jr. handsome, brilliant, example to all, killed in plane as was Kathleen, who had she lived, would have been the top social leader in the younger set in England, but neither she nor her husband lived. Jack with an ideal life, compatible, intellectually as well as socially, was unexpectedly assassinated. Bob and Ethel, ideally matched socially and temperamentally . . . talented, happy, young, assassinated.*
>
> *But God or "destiny" just does not allow a family to exist which has all these star-studded adornments. Ted, too, has everything and may even be president, at least he should be successful and happy. I myself am quite reconciled to the fact that I could not anticipate an ideal successful life.*

I cannot find in literature or in life many people whose lives we envy. Most of course proceed on a middling course, not many great thrills—the normal number of deaths and disappointments. Often read Hecuba's "Lament on the Death of her Grandson," written by Euripides when she spoke of Fortune— "Here now, there now, she springs back again, an idiot's dance," and what was true in 550 B.C. is so true now.[2]

Rose experienced tremendous loss and guilt and had regrets, but those emotions did not prevent her from living a full life. Perhaps, emboldened by her confirmation as papal countess, Rose came to rely on her faith in God to cope with so much loss. In fact, it was her unwavering faith in God that allowed her to reconcile in her heart that some situations were not within her control, and so while she grieved deeply, her life was never without meaning and purpose.

It is common to experience guilt and regret when you are caring for your loved one and to revisit those feelings again should you experience loss. From a psychological standpoint, guilt and regret are closely related, and although they have slightly different meanings, the definitions are often intermingled.

Regret is frequently attributed to something that you feel you could have done but in truth the situation was beyond your control, whereas guilt is associated with the contradictory internal feelings resulting from thoughts about what you should have done based on the insight you had at the time or subsequently. In some situations, *guilt* and *regret* can act as immobilizers, because you simply do not know how to move forward.

Should you find that you are feeling guilty or experiencing regret, please consider reviewing the suggestions included in the chapter "You've Committed No Offense in Surviving," which focuses on guilt. "The Transfer of Hope" chapter is dedicated to working through regret.

Your overarching takeaway with both emotions is that experiencing some measure of guilt or regret is healthy, specifically when the purpose is to reflect and make changes for the future, but it is also important that you are mindful not to dwell on either your guilt or your regrets.

Acknowledge your feelings

What events or situations would you like to look back on as having done to complete satisfaction? Now having pondered this and having made a list of these things, pick one or two and plan to do each one without a trace of regret. Every now and then, return to the list and add to it, if necessary.

_____
_____
_____
_____
_____
_____
_____
_____
_____
_____
_____
_____
_____

Write the name of the person or persons toward whom you feel some level of guilt. Beside each name, write down what action or behavior it was that you feel guilty about. What feelings arise in you when you think about the person or event? Next make a note of how long you have felt this way. Finally, search your soul for a way to forgive yourself, even if it just means acknowledging your human spirit. Then practice the act of forgiveness as best you can and let go of your feelings of guilt.

_____
_____
_____
_____
_____
_____

Stay open to being Inspired

Many people are driven by guilt. They spend their entire lives running from regrets and hiding their shame. Guilt-driven people are manipulated by their memories. They allow their past to control their future. They often unconsciously punish themselves by sabotaging their own success.

—Richard Warren [3]

Dr. Eboni Ivory Green

Reflect deeply so that you can heal

Never forget the three powerful resources you always have available to you: love, prayer, and forgiveness.

—H. Jackson Brown Jr.[4]

---

[1]Kevin Cullen, "Finding Her Way in the Clan: Diaries, Letters Reveal a More Complex Kennedy Matriarch," *New York Times,* 2007, http://archive.boston.com/news/local/articles/2007/05/13/finding_her_way_in_the_clan/. Accessed September 29, 2016.

[2]Gerald O'Brien, "Rosemary Kennedy: The Importance of a Historical Footnote," *Journal of Family History* 29, no. 3 (2004): 225–36.

[3]Richard Warren, *The Purpose-Driven Life: What on Earth Am I Here For?* (Grand Rapids, Mich.: Zondervan, 2002).

[4] H. Jackson Brown, Jr.. BrainyQuote.com, Xplore Inc, 2016. https://www.brainyquote.com/quotes/authors/h/h_jackson_brown_jr.html, accessed September 29, 2016.

Work by Day and Sleep at Night?

I find myself awake once again, unable to settle into the comforts, warmth, and protection of my pillow-filled bed. I find myself roaming the halls, searching each room, looking to see that nothing is out of place. I hear the sweet sounds of snores coming from my family sleeping soundly, nuzzled in their favorite blankets. I am surfing the channels knowing late-night television is like an empty promise that always goes unfulfilled. So my insomnia persists while others are able to rest their minds, clear their heads, and welcome beautiful rest. My mind is tired of replaying scenarios, so I place all in His hands and ask Him to comfort me with His unwavering strength and, tonight, allow my mind, body, and spirit to get some rest.

—Dr. Eboni Ivory Green

President Abraham Lincoln was not only the Great Emancipator, he was also the poster child for depression and insomnia. The source of his melancholy has been documented in detail—it has been almost unanimously attributed to the loss of his mother at the age of nine, his sister in 1928, and a close friend, Ann Rutledge, when he was a young man. His angst likely culminated during his presidency with the death of his son Willie and the six hundred thousand Americans who perished in the Civil War.

However, it appears as though Lincoln's inability to fall asleep crept in without warning. Who wouldn't have had difficulty unwinding with so many losses and when the world was in such turmoil? If you take into consideration that the purpose of sleep is to relax while having little or no conscious thought,[1] it is easy to conclude why rest did not come easy. I would bet that, like most individuals who have trouble falling asleep, he began by experiencing a few restless nights and, before he knew it, was suffering from chronic insomnia.

When he was unable to sleep during the years of the Civil War, Lincoln would pace the White House long past midnight. His habitual sleeplessness spilled over to others, in particular John Hay, who was his personal secretary. The president would keep awake by telling Hay funny stories and "reading Shakespeare, the end of Henry VIII and the beginning of Richard III, late into the night until his heavy eyelids caught his considerate notice and he sent him to bed."[2]

I believe that Vachel Lindsay captures the true essence of Lincoln's habitual sleeplessness in the following poem:

> *It is portentous, and a thing of state. That here at midnight, in our little town a mourning figure walks, and will not rest, near the old court-house pacing up and down. Or by his homestead, or in shadowed yards, he lingers where his children used to play, or through the market, on the well-worn stones he stalks until the dawn-stars burn away.*
>
> *A bronzed, lank man! His suit of ancient black, a famous high top-hat and plain worn shawl make him the quaint great figure that men love, the prairie-lawyer, master of us all. He cannot sleep upon his hillside now. He is among us:—as in times before! And we who toss and lie awake for long breathe deep, and start, to see him pass the door.*
>
> *His head is bowed. He thinks on men and kings. Yea, when the*

sick world cries, how can he sleep? Too many peasants fight, they know not why, too many homesteads in black terror weep. The sins of all the war-lords burn his heart. He sees the dreadnaughts scouring every man. He carries on his shawl-wrapped shoulders now the bitterness, the folly and the pain. He cannot rest until a spirit-dawn shall come;—the shining hope of Europe free; the league of sober folk, the Workers' Earth, bringing long peace to Cornland, Alp and Sea.

It breaks his heart that kings must murder still, that all his hours of travail here for men seem yet in vain. And who will bring white peace that he may sleep upon his hill again?[3]

Lincoln appears to have worked himself to the bone, fretted and worried endlessly, slept very little, and at times endured intense sorrow. Similar to most who are grieving, he worked by day but he didn't sleep at night.

To the contrary, he was only able to quiet his mind after having taken long walks late at night, reading correspondences from concerned citizens well into the evening, and thrusting himself into great literary works until he was so tired that he had no choice other than to sleep. Even then, Lincoln had strange and often prophetic dreams so that he was never truly unwinding, nor did he experience paradoxical sleep.

Inadequate sleep long-term is directly correlated with substantial distress and increased mortality. One need only look at pictures shared by Jesus Diaz[4] to visualize the significantly worn and aged appearance of Lincoln in a photo taken in 1865 as compared to one taken in 1858, just seven years earlier. The former displays a man who was beyond exhausted and who appears to be twenty, maybe thirty years older.

Should you find yourself worried, confused, and in a general fog, in the early days, weeks, and months following the loss of your loved one—you are not alone. Approximately one-third of adults have trouble falling and/or staying asleep, absent of grief. The good news is that sleep is widely considered a modifiable behavior, meaning that by identifying the cause of your insomnia and making minor changes, you have the opportunity to improve your ability to sleep through the night. The following are tips that you may consider if you find that you are having difficulty falling and staying asleep.

Rest. Since your sleep pattern will likely be altered following the loss of your loved one, it is important to rest when you are able, at least short term. Napping is not a suggested long-term approach as it is likely to further interrupt your ability to sleep through the night. However, what is most important during the immediate days and weeks is that you have an opportunity to replenish. Not doing so is problematic, as the lack of sleep will likely thwart your emotional and physical healing.

You may find that taking an occasional nap is the best way for you to replenish your strength. Lincoln was known to take advantage of downtime, and while it does not appear that he napped much, he did lounge to read the paper and to reflect from time to time. In fact, in his early years, when he was a young lawyer, Lincoln is said to have come in first thing in the morning and found a comfortable spot to lie down so that his feet were elevated, and there he would read the daily news.

Set a routine that includes self-care practices prior to going to bed. Sleep hygiene begins with setting a routine and ensuring that you have a comfortable place to sleep. Your daily routine might include going to sleep around the same time each night. You might also make sure your bed and pillows are comfortable, as a bed or pillows that are too hard or too soft could leave you feeling like Goldilocks on an endless search to find a bed that is just right.

Adjusting the temperature in your bedroom so that it is pleasant could also be an effective approach. You will likely not fall asleep in an environment that is too hot or too cold. Some also find that taking a warm bath and drinking warm milk or a non-stimulating tea does the trick because these practices make the body cooler and more relaxed.

Clear your mind. Sometimes there are so many thoughts and worries swirling in your mind that unless you clear your thoughts, you will likely not fall asleep. If you find that you are in bed awake for twenty minutes or more, try clearing your mind by journaling or participating in another activity until you are able to sleep. The following are suggested approaches that you might incorporate into your daily routine so that you can clear your mind before bed:

Journaling about something positive every evening before you go to bed is a way to end your day on a high note. You might jot down three to five things from that day for which you're thankful. Then take a day out of the month and review your list.

Journaling your dreams. It is normal to experience strange dreams, thoughts, and sensations following the loss of your loved one. Journaling your dreams may help you to identify common themes, as sometimes your dreams are representative of your subconscious worries.

Write out your worries. Should you find that you are having trouble with replaying past words or actions in your head, consider making a worry box. When a thought comes to mind, write it down and place it in the worry box. Give yourself a week or two, and then open the box. Completing this exercise may assist you in identifying common themes for your worries and lead to specific actions that you can take to make changes in the future.

Use meditation as a way to clear your mind. When my grandmother passed away, I experienced insomnia. I did not know about the benefits of meditation at the time, so I used my love of classical music as a way to unwind before bed. You might try listening to music without words, you could find guided imagery effective, or perhaps you have a method of meditation that you can learn from reading. Remember that the goal of meditation is to clear your mind so that your heart and soul can become one; in doing so, you will be able to relax your body so that you can fall asleep.

Unplug an hour before bed. Cell phones, computers, and the television should be turned off at least an hour before your bedtime as they can impact your circadian rhythm. Consider replacing your time on the phone or the computer, a least an hour before bed, with a self-care strategy that will help you unwind.

Reach out to your doctor. Should you find that your insomnia persists for three weeks or longer, you feel that you are not rested after sleep, or you wake in the middle of the night without the ability to go back to sleep, you might consider reaching out to your doctor. There are an estimated ninety sleep disorders and even more comorbidities associated with a lack of sleep. Therefore it is prudent to talk with your doctor about any challenges you are having regarding sleep.

There is a relationship between sleep quality, bereavement, and depression. All we need to do is look to President Lincoln and remember his worn appearance in 1865 to recognize that good sleep accompanies successful bereavement. Do all that you can to get the rest you need!

Acknowledge your feelings

Please list two or three ways to quiet your mind before bedtime.

_____
_____
_____
_____
_____

Take a moment to think back to a special time when you felt a profound if not divine connection to the universe—a moment that transcended your everyday feelings and responsibilities. Try to recall the essence of what you experienced. Then open your eyes and try to recapture the event on paper in as much detail as possible. You might consider using what you write to draft a meditation or a prayer.

_____
_____
_____
_____
_____

Dr. Eboni Ivory Green

Stay open to being Inspired

The body needs its rest, and sleep is extremely important in any health regimen. There should be three main things: eating, exercise, and sleep. All three together in the right balance make for a truly healthy lifestyle.

—Rohit Shetty[5]

Reflect deeply so that you can heal

You may think you can keep moving at a rapid pace and catch up on your sleep later down the road. I have never seen that happen. Either you end up sleeping too much, and you are tired; or you do not get enough sleep and you are exhausted!

---

[1]Merriam-Webster.com, s.v. "sleep," http://www.merriam-webster.com/dictionary/sleep., accessed September 29, 2016

[2]David Wallechinsky and Irving Wallace. Reproduced with permission from "The People's Almanac" series of books (1975–81).

[3]Vachel Lindsay, "Abraham Lincoln Walks at Midnight," http://www.poetryfoundation.org/poems-and-poets/poems/detail/47372, accessed September 29, 2016.

[4]Jesus Diaz, "Before and after the War: The Dramatic Aging of Abraham Lincoln," 2014, http://sploid.gizmodo.com/before-and-after-the-presidency-the-dramatic-aging-of-1530050410, accessed September 29, 2016.

[5]Rohit Shetty. BrainyQuote.com, Xplore Inc, 2016. https://www.brainyquote.com/quotes/authors/r/rohit_shetty.html, accessed September 29, 2016.

Heavy Raindrops

I will cry real tears, the type of tears that bring forth healing. These real tears are sometimes heavy like drops of rain falling during a spring thunderstorm, the tears fill my room till it seems my bed will float in a river of healing tears. While floating down the river of healing tears the rage of the water flows, surging forward through the twists and turns of this teary river. Sometimes others observe the surge and how they want help but, they do not understand how this river of tears frees me. For through the tears my heart is opened and my feelings are released. These tears flow sometimes like a mist and fall one at a time, slowly and steadily, they drop slowly on my pillow but the moisture only touches the pillow's surface. Others wish to comfort me because they do not understand I am forever comforted through these real tears.

—Dr. Eboni Green

One morning in November as I was getting the children ready for school I walked into the kitchen and found my sixteen-year-old daughter having a grand maul seizure. Until that morning she had been the picture of health, so we were very scared.

We immediately called 911 and were rushed to the emergency room. My daughter and I were together from the moment I found her having the seizure until she was escorted to the room where they were to perform an MRI. Alone, for the first time that morning, I found that

I was no longer able to contain my sadness and fear so I started to cry. My emotional release was not quiet or pretty, but I thought I was all alone. I was crying, praying for strength, so I didn't hold back anything.

Just as I was feeling the most vulnerable a cleaning lady appeared out of nowhere and without saying a word she opened a box of tissues and handed me one. She waited for me to regain my composure and then she touched my hand and gave me the box. This kind soul was not uncomfortable with my tears, she let me cry. I was comforted by her act of kindness and silent presence.

I am a firm believer in the healing power of an emotional release. I think it is important to cry when you feel like crying, ventilate when you are feeling angry, and when you are happy laugh as hard as you can. It is simply unhealthy to keep your feelings bottled up. In fact, if you are holding them in it could be an indicator that you have not fully accepted, acknowledged, or coped with the loss of your loved one.

What is an Emotional Release?

An emotional release is an unburdening of the soul that is thought to have healing power. It often begins with shedding tears, but usually tension and stress is released and emotional resolution achieved. Emotional resolution, the end result of an emotional release is accompanied by healing after you have faced the gravity of your loss.

Furthermore, emotional resolution can be defined as an outward expression of inner tension and raw emotions being alleviated. An emotional release and subsequently emotional resolution can occur spontaneously, however, what is particularly important is that you have an opportunity to express your sadness without having to explain your feelings.

It should be noted that an emotional release and subsequent emotional resolution is experienced in a variety of ways and that what is healing or therapeutic to you might not be healing for someone else.

Not wanting to face your sadness

You might need the encouragement of others to release your emotions especially if you have not faced your sadness. In fact, it is not uncommon to not have had the opportunity to take an inventory of your emotions as your focus has probably been meeting the needs of your loved one while he or she was still living.

You may not want to face your sadness, because while it can be empowering, it can also be scary. You may also feel afraid of expressing your feelings because facing your sadness also means that you may have to confront deep questions regarding the meaning and purpose of life and your mortality. Another reason you may not want to face your sadness is the fear of being swept away by your emotions which is entirely possible, natural, and okay.

The truth is your tears have healing potential as they remove toxic substances, help you release emotional stress, and restore your health. It is not only important to release your tears but to understand the cleansing effect of releasing your emotions has on any internal turmoil you may be experiencing.

It is particularly special when you take the opportunity to share your grief with those in your inner circle. In fact, social support is a part of the catharsis that may help you to express your raw emotions. Whenever possible, it is important that you take advantage of the opportunity to express your sadness in an environment where you feel that others are not judging or minimizing your feelings.

Even if you do not want to cry or experience an emotional release, in front of others for a variety of reasons, fear, embarrassment, helplessness, and the need to stay strong it is important that you not suppress how you are feeling. Not expressing yourself can be a distancing and I can say from experience that it does not make you feel better.

If you find that you are holding in your feelings it may be important for you to let others know that you need the permission to cry and that they need not do anything to prevent you from sharing your tears. In fact, expressing your emotions with others and receiving emotional support is cleansing.

It is healthy to share your sadness because you give others the opportunity to empathize with you. You benefit personally via the empathy, sympathy, and or comfort that others bless you with; your loved ones, family, or friends benefit from strengthened social bonds and from being able to exhibit empathy. In essence, others can attempt to feel your pain.

For example, one of the first times I expressed my grief about my daughter was while I was giving a lecture about grief. Just as I completed my introduction and was about to open up the discussion I looked over and caught a glimpse of a young lady who had recently lost her father. She was sobbing. She was fully expressing her sadness.

As she cried another young lady sat and held her tight, rocking her slowly and gently. There were more than twenty individuals in the room yet no one tried to keep her from expressing her sadness. We just allowed her to release everything she was holding deep inside. Sometimes the best thing you can do is to say nothing and instead simply be silently present.

I know that I found it helpful to release my sadness through tears in the hospital room when my daughter Asia was diagnosed with a brain tumor. The young lady who was grieving the loss of her father also found it cleansing to freely express her sadness through tears with a small group of caregivers.

While it is important to release your emotions, it is equally important to note that if you find that you are often crying alone. Suppressing tears because of shame or embarrassment it is not healthy. Also, if you find that you are crying daily, for an extended period of time (six months or longer), or if crying interferes with daily life, it is not healthy and perhaps there is more meaning behind your tears.

Reaching out for help might be important if you feel overwhelmed by your feelings or if your grief is complicated. Remember that getting in tune with your sadness will not destroy you. To the contrary, paying attention to your emotions may afford you the opportunity to work through your grief in a controlled manner so that it does not resurface in an unhealthy manner later down the road.

What is most important is that you give yourself permission to experience an emotional release and reach out for support when necessary. Seek the assistance of a professional grief counselor should you find that you are in need of the help to work through your grief. Your goal is emotional resolution.

Acknowledge your feelings

Has there been a time when you were overcome with feelings of grief? Combing your memory, can you remember a time when you were told not to act a certain way? Take a moment to describe this incident.

_____

_____

_____

_____

_____

Stay open to being **In***spired*

Tears have a way of putting life in perspective. They can actually help you to laugh again. How can I be crying in the morning and laughing with my friends in the afternoon? A young woman asked. This bridge-building from sorrow to joy is one of the gifts tears offer.

They help you put your loss in a special place. You don't forget your loved one or your loss, but you are freed to live.

–Mildred Tengbom [1]

R*eflect deeply so that you can heal*

Some of my best or most healing tears came in the car in the hospital parking lot where I was completely alone. I did not have to explain my tears and I could sob and sob. I took full advantage of this time to cry.

---

[1] Mildred Tengbom, *When your Spouse Dies*, (Minneapolis: Augsburg Fortress Publishers, 1990) [page 25].

Remembering You Makes Me Smile

When I remember your face, your loving embrace, the time that we shared, the comforting words spoken with such grace, I can't help but feel the corner of my lips turn up and a smile comes across my face. I have been sad for a while, too many days to count, trying hard not to forget our spiritual connection. Sometimes the days are long and the evenings seem even longer, but nothing comforts me so much as the memory of you, because remembering you makes me smile.

—Dr. Eboni Ivory Green

My Aunt Cynthia had a laugh that was infectious. Her hearty chuckle and lighthearted semantics frequently left me in hysterics. Sometimes I simply could not believe what she was telling me and would laugh so hard that my eyes filled with happy tears. Her tall tales, intertwined with historical truths, were not only hilarious but also insightful.

On more than one occasion, I had the opportunity to gain perspective on an obscure but meaningful tidbit that proved useful down the road. I won't romanticize our relationship; there were times when Aunt Cynthia drove me absolutely crazy with the nuances and peccadilloes that accompanied her mental illness.

One of her more embarrassing (for me) but favorite (for her) adventures involved going to Target or Walmart, where she would shop for hours with the full knowledge that she didn't have the money to pay for all of the items that she was placing in her cart. An equally gratifying activity was for Aunt Cynthia to put each item on the checkout conveyer, slowly and one at a time, so that the cashier had to ring up each item at a snail's pace.

Yet, her greatest satisfaction was to inform the now worn-out cashier that she did not have the money to pay for everything. With the line now held up and likely quite lengthy, my dear aunt would have the cashier remove one item off of the bill at a time until she reached an amount that was agreeable. It was so embarrassing!

I watched Aunt Cynthia do this once or twice before I simply intervened during subsequent shopping trips by paying for everything. But even then, she would find a way to return unwanted items and get a small refund so that she could shop again. Later, I realized that it was therapeutic for her to get out and socialize, to buy something even if she didn't really need or want it. Aunt Cynthia enjoyed the undivided attention of the cashier and the customers in the line waiting for her to locate her money or return receipt, which was always at the very bottom of her clutter-filled purse. In retrospect, it was funny—kind of.

In 1999, I relocated to Nebraska from my hometown, so I didn't take Aunt Cynthia to the store very often. Within a year, she moved to a small city in Kansas and our shopping trips stopped altogether. With the distance between us, she took to writing me letters.

From time to time, I would go to the mailbox and there would be a letter from her. I would smile and say to my husband, "Oh, look, I have a letter from Aunt Cynthia." Each correspondence consisted of several pages with a few quick thoughts or words of encouragement and was accompanied by nickels, quarters, dimes, and pennies taped to the final page. But what I found to be most endearing was that each letter concluded with a question about when we might see one another again.

I read each page quietly, except when I laughed about something she had written, and then shared the particularly interesting highlights with my husband. After reading each one, I would put the letters away with the quarters and pennies intact and tuck them in a private place. I loved reading her letters; in fact, I saved every single one.

Aunt Cynthia had a pure heart, so she had everything! She always found a way to freely share her sense of humor and her lightheartedness with me and anyone who was willing and accepting of her love. When she died, I truly felt in my heart in some symbolic way that all my happiness had been taken away. For a time my heart was so heavy that I didn't have the courage to acknowledge how much I missed her laughter and ended up placing myself on some type of laughter timeout because she was gone. Simply put, I stopped laughing for a time, or at least it felt as if I did.

The anatomy of laughter

Then, one day, a thought popped into my head and stimulated chemicals in my brain that triggered a response deep within my soul. I heard a familiar sound and realized that it had originated from within—I was laughing again. I am sure I was thinking about something my aunt had said or done, and although I was all alone, I laughed so hard that I cried, and then I laughed again. And do you know what? I realized that laughing was one of the best things I could do to cope with my grief.

Dr. Madan Kataria states that "laughter exercises coupled with deep breathing changes the physiology, thereby changing the mood state and helping a person to view the situation differently. It is a cathartic exercise which helps release pent up feelings and makes people emotionally balanced."[1] As a result of my personal experience, I have come to believe that nothing beats a good, hearty laugh that originates from deep within.

After loss, you will likely not feel much like laughing, or you may simply need something to stimulate your funny bone. The following are suggestions that I found helpful when I found that I had stopped laughing.

Make a notebook that comprises your favorite jokes, photographs, letters, or anything else that brings a smile to your face. Even though it has been a few years now since she passed, I have not felt emotionally brave enough to compile all of my Aunt Cynthia's letters, but when I am emotionally ready, I intend to place them in a notebook, especially the really funny ones.

Herbert Lefcourt shares, "If I were to guess which form of humor will be found to have the greatest importance for us as a means of coping with stressors, it would be perspective-taking humor, the kind of humor that allows us to have distance from our own experiences so that ultimately we enjoy this 'gift' of not having to take either our failures or successes too seriously."[2] For me, the letters are a gift that I plan to enjoy. You might decide that a combination of funny photos, jokes, and other mementos stimulates happy thoughts. Revisiting your notebook when you are feeling particularly down or having a challenging day may in fact lift your spirits.

Hold storytelling evenings with others who were close to your loved one. My sister-in-law Kaye was magnetic! All she needed to do was walk in the room, and before you could resist her gregarious personality, you were having the time of your life. She was so much fun, all the time! One of the ways my sister-in-law Nikki (Sis) and I cope with Kaye no longer being with us is to tell funny stories about the times we shared.

It is the little things that she would say or do at family gatherings that make me smile. Sometimes Sis and I laugh, and sometimes we cry. But sharing helps keep Kaye's memory alive. Melinda Palacio uses poetic storytelling to remember her mother's laughter. Perhaps Melinda's poem could serve as inspiration to tell your loved one's story:

> *The story of my mother touches the wind and rattles me off balance, raises the small hairs on my forearms, my skin no longer feels my own. I long to be cradled by a cloud, suspended and sheltered. I listen to the words of my Grandmother Spirit. My elder says look beneath your skin and you'll see the loneliness in your veins. I hear drumming, a familiar wail of pain. The drums stop. The story is as ordinary as once upon a time there was a happy woman who lived a short life before dying, leaving behind a daughter. The pages between the beginning and the end are filled with laughter. A girl with wild hair the color of the Rio Grande sinks to her feet into the muddy river and says, you laugh like my grandmother. I laugh harder because the wild woman is my mother.*[3]

Once you have written your story, don't forget to share it. You might read it aloud and ask your family members to expand or add to it and then keep it in your notebook to revisit every now and again.

Make a list of two or three comedies (with the intention of seeing them again). Kevin Hart's comedy special *Laugh at My Pain* lends credence to the importance of humor as a coping strategy following the loss of a loved one. In Kevin's standup routine, he artfully shares his and his brother's experience with caring for their mom following her diagnosis with terminal cancer. Not only is his humor deeply relatable, but also it reminds you of the importance of humor in spite of your pain. Kevin models how laughter is not only healthy but necessary. You might select a few comedies to watch and rotate them based on how you are feeling. The idea is that the comedy should give you a break from your thoughts so that you can simply open your heart to positive emotions.

Consider visiting people and places when you need to lift your spirits. Changing your location can also change your disposition. Perhaps you could plan to visit a special friend or a place that brings you comfort. If you do not have someone with whom you might travel, perhaps there is a travel group that you could join for your dream trip. In the long term, being around others is important. Plus, you never know what you will hear, see, or say that will spark your humor.

Uncovering your funny side after losing your loved one is easily overlooked, and before you know it, you have lost your joy. Do not allow yourself to become too busy, feel guilty, or close yourself off from feeling happy. Instead, stay open to happy moments in the midst of your sorrow. It took me some time to feel comfortable with freely laughing again when my aunt died.

But then, one night, my husband made a trip to Walmart to purchase some aluminum foil. Sounds simple enough, right? He grabbed the foil and got in line. There was one lane open, but there was just one gentleman ahead of him in the line. He waited patiently, but when the cashier finished ringing up the items, which totaled well over three-hundred dollars, the gentleman said he didn't have any money.

My husband smiled and moved to the next line as the manager and the cashier started to void the order and unbag all of the groceries. He came straight home and said, "I just ran into someone who reminded me of your aunt." He told me the story, and we had a good, hearty laugh. I felt like it was her way of telling me that it was okay to experience joy again, and I was thankful, because for a time I didn't think it was possible.

Acknowledge your feelings

Are there moments you can recall (with your loved one) that are so funny that the mere thought puts a grin or a smile on your face?

_____
_____
_____
_____

Keep your notebook on hand so that when you are having a bad day, you can pull it out to help you regain some emotional balance.

*Stay open to being **Inspired***

A smile starts on the lips, a grin spreads to the eyes, a chuckle comes from the belly; but a good laugh bursts forth from the soul, overflows, and bubbles all around.

—Carolyn Birmingham[4]

Reflect deeply so that you can heal

When you recall past experiences, they can be either vivid or dusky. Dusky memories are frequently task oriented. These memories fade as time progresses because they are not emotionally based. In direct contrast, vivid memories are generally emotionally based and relate to your life experiences, the people you know, and the good times you shared together. You will have memories associated with the tasks you perform, but tasks do not necessarily make long-lasting memories. So I say, laugh as much and as hard as you can. In doing so, you will make memories that last forever.

---

[1] Madan Kataria, Laughter Yoga International, http://www.laughter.org/, accessed on September 29, 2016.

[2] C. R. Snyder, *Coping with Stress* (Cary: Oxford University Press, 2001).

[3] Melinda Palacio, "Laughter," *Black Renaissance* 8, no. 2 (2008): 152, 191.

[4] Carolyn Birmingham, "120 Inspirational Quotes about Laughter," http://www.laughteronlineuniversity.com/120-quotes-laughter-throughout-history/, accessed on September 29, 2016.

You Do Not Need to Walk Alone

She sat and cried, and when she finished she felt better. She had been grieving alone, and to grieve alone is a lonely place to be. No one understood her pain, the sorrows hidden deep within, and the torture of being alone in her despair. To suffer in silence, to grieve alone, now that is a lonely place to be.

—Dr. Eboni Green

I embarked on the journey of writing *Reflections* with a solid understanding that it is natural to feel lonely when you lose someone you love. Yet, for me, the surety of this fact was not fully fortified until I ceased to shield my heart from the truth and honestly embraced my personal tendency to avoid people, places, and situations to cope with my sadness.

Subsequent intensive introspection further led me to fully acknowledge that although taking the opportunity to reflect is healthy, it is important to be careful that you do not limit your interactions to the point that you are lonely and isolated. For me the tendency is to rely on avoidance as a coping strategy by definition, avoidance is to steer clear of activities that might trigger memories or cause you to deal with your feelings head-on. My avoiding ended up being a major contributing factor to the perception that it was okay for me to walk alone. Jeanette Winterson's poem captures the essence of the art of avoidance coping:

Living with life is very hard. Mostly we do our best to stifle life—to be tame or to be wanton. To be tranquilized or raging. Extremes have the same effect; they insulate us from the intensity of life. And extremes—whether of dullness or fury—successfully prevent feeling. I know our feelings can be so unbearable that we employ ingenious strategies—unconscious strategies—to keep those feelings away.

We do a feelings-swap, where we avoid feeling sad or lonely or afraid or inadequate, and feel angry instead. It can work the other way, too—sometimes you do need to feel angry, not inadequate; sometimes you do need to feel love and acceptance, and not the tragic drama of your life.

It takes courage to feel the feeling—and not trade it on the feelings-exchange, or even transfer it altogether to another person. You know how in couples one person is always doing all the weeping or the raging while the other one seems so calm and reasonable? I understood that feelings were difficult for me although I was overwhelmed by them.[1]

Do you feel as though you are using avoidance as a strategy to cope with the loss of your loved one? If the answer is yes, you will likely find that by avoiding addressing your feelings today, you are inadvertently contributing to increased levels of anxiety that you will likely have to deal with later down the road. In essence, you run the risk of complicating your grief and prolonging your angst.

What are you avoiding?

Family and friends. The Fourth of July is a particularly festive holiday for me and my husband. The year before my father-in-law, Johnny, passed away, we had more than fifty family members make their way to our house for the celebration. We had much to eat and drink, but the highlight of the night was the huge fireworks show put on for the children.

Later that year, in November, we lost two sisters, Kaye and Chrissy; in January, my father-in-law; and two uncles in the spring. By the time we made it to the next year's Fourth of July, none of us felt up to celebrating, but the family got together and enjoyed the day. Our family took every opportunity to see one another for birthdays, holidays, and an occasional Sunday dinner. Yet, deep inside, I felt as though we were missing an entire table of family members so that it became increasingly difficult for me to want to socialize at family gatherings.

Yes, I would cook, clean, organize, greet each guest—and then promptly retreat to a secluded area to watch a movie, work, or do anything to avoid socializing. It took a couple of years before I recognized that I was isolating myself from the family to avoid being reminded of the loved ones we had lost.

Cities, towns, or other special places. I grew up traveling the world because my dad was in the military, but Sioux City, Iowa, was my home base. Both my grandmothers Frankie and Gran, Aunt Cynthia, my sister Rochelle, and my stepmother, Doris, all now passed, lived there. Over the years, I began to recognize that most of my visits back to Iowa were emotionally distressing. I began to connect going to Iowa with attending yet another funeral of someone whom I loved dearly. Without realizing it, I started avoiding visiting my hometown altogether.

Avoiding things. My grandmother's afghan brings me comfort as I always feel closer to her when I curl up with it or one of the children is wrapped in it fast asleep. Yet you may find that as a result of your grief, you are avoiding mementos that remind you of the love you shared with someone that added meaning to your life. The challenge then becomes holding on to the items but keeping them tucked away so that you are not enjoying the items. When you do this, perhaps you are suppressing the special memories attached to the items, and that is not living.

It can be very frightening to face your internal fears head-on, and if you are not careful, before you know it, you will have shut down like me. You will stop visiting places and indeed close yourself off from your memories all in an effort to protect the sanctity of what has been normal in your life.

I freely acknowledge that if I had not been writing about isolation, I would not have concluded I was avoiding people and places because of my grief.

Should you find that you are moving toward an avoidance strategy for coping, you are really only kicking the can of sadness further down the road. In time, you will likely come to the conclusion that it is far healthier to work through your sadness as it comes. I can tell you personally that a buildup of grief only leads to a meltdown—it is not fun, nor is it healthy. Rather than isolating and avoiding, you are encouraged to reconnect with friends and family who have been there to support you. Learn to share your feelings, as your loved ones will not know how you feel unless you are willing to share. Do not to allow your life to become empty when you are surrounded by people who love you. It is my sincere desire that you begin to take the necessary steps to open your heart so that you can create new moments, keeping in mind that living does not mean that you are in any way forgetting the special memories shared between you and your loved one who has passed.

*A*cknowledge your feelings

What do you do to nurture the connections between you and your family or friends? In other words, how are you a good friend to others?

_____
_____
_____
_____
_____

What is it that keeps your bonds of friendship strong, and what lets some friendships fade away?

_____
_____
_____
_____
_____

Make a list of three new places where you can go to begin to meet new people as possible members of your network of support.

_____
_____
_____
_____
_____

Dr. Eboni Ivory Green

*Stay open to being **In**spired*

Negative emotions like loneliness, envy, and guilt have an important role to play in a happy life; they're big, flashing signs that something needs to change.

—Gretchen Rubin[2]

***R**eflect deeply so that you can heal*

*No man is an island, entire of itself; every man is a piece
of the continent, a part of the main.
If a clod be washed away
by the sea, Europe is the less,
as well as if a promontory were,
as well as if a manor of thy friend's or of thine own were:
any man's death diminishes me, because I am involved in
mankind, and therefore never send to know for whom the
bells tolls;
it tolls for thee.*

—John Donne[3]

---

[1] Jeanette Winterson, *Why Be Happy When You Could Be Normal* (Canada: Knopf, 2012).

[2] Gretchen Rubin. BrainyQuote.com, Xplore Inc, 2016. http://www.brainyquote.com/quotes/authors/g/gretchen_rubin.html, accessed September 27, 2016.

[3] John Donne, "No Man Is an Island—A Selection from the Prose," 1970, http://www.goodreads.com/work/quotes/6791114-no-man-is-an-island, accessed September 27, 2016

Being Mindful

I remember a time when things were less complicated. I remember simpler times when the company of another filled my time and occupied my heart. A time when I looked at caring for another and that caring really defined me.

I remember a time when sharing myself was a true expression of my love and devotion. So during this trying time, I wonder if an opportunity will present itself for me to feel again. For today I find myself numb to the human experience and devoid of emotion. I wonder if happier days filled with vibrant colors cascading in the summer breeze will return. Will I have the opportunity to once again be carefree?

I envision a time when life was less complicated and today I would have to say I miss those times. I miss the times when I was a virgin to guilt and grief and only understood their definitions described in literary dictionaries. Deep inside, I hate to admit my feelings of frustration, and so I bury my feelings deep within.

I envision a time when things were less complicated, but the more I grieve, the further away this uncompounded life seems.

—Dr. Eboni Green

One of the most valuable lessons I have learned as a caregiver is that change is inevitable and adaptation is necessary! In fact, I would bet that even in your grief, you are cognizant of the pointlessness of trying to resist your personal evolution and that, even now, transforming challenging problems into manageable solutions is one of the more consistent facets of your pilgrimage.

American hiker and itinerant traveler Christopher McCandless, known for his sojourn where he hitchhiked to Alaska, poignantly highlights that "the joy of life comes from our encounters with new experiences, and hence there is no greater joy than to have an endlessly changing horizon, for each day to have a new and different sun."[1]

Yet even when you embrace change, it does not mean that your willingness to adapt will be devoid of psychological consequences, namely, that excessive rejigging is emotionally distressing. To that end, I think that it is vital to consider taking an inventory of your stress, your distress, and evaluating the possibility that you may have a post-traumatic stress response, especially during the weeks and months following the loss of your loved one.

I think of my mother-in-law, Emma, who has been living alone ever since my father-in-law passed away two years ago. Emma is no longer able to live alone, and I privately worry about her ability to cope with the numerous life-altering events she has endured in the past couple of years.

Yet my more pressing concerns stem from the possibility that my husband, sister-in-law, and brother-in-law are at risk for post-traumatic grief response simply because they have waxed and waned between stress and distress for the past two years, beginning with losing two of their sisters in the same week as well as their father.

Terrence along with his sister and brother have become full-time caregivers for their mother. Famed British philosopher Allen Watts says that "the only way to make sense out of change is to plunge into it, move with it, and join the dance."[2]

Making minor life changes is generally fairly inconsequential and only briefly adds to your stress. However, major life changes have far-reaching consequences, and without getting too technical, it is the pileup of stressors that can result in a post-traumatic response to grief. Increasing evidence suggests that grieving caregivers are at risk for developing post-traumatic stress disorder (PTSD).

Should you find that you are experiencing continued stress, distress, or anxiety or feel that you might be having a post-traumatic stress response to your grief, please consider reviewing the chapter "A Quiet Mind." The chapter offers suggestions for identifying and coping with the aforementioned emotions, including when you might consider reaching out for help.

Once your immediate needs are addressed and when you are feeling secure emotionally, my long-term wish is that you open yourself to the possibility of post-traumatic growth. Growing after a post-traumatic experience may sound like an oxymoron, but it is a real possibility that involves embracing your power through mindfulness—opening your heart so that you identify a renewed purpose and the opportunity to achieve self-actualization.

Being mindful. My grandmother was an avid reader of *Guideposts* magazine, which is where I think she first read the words to the song "O Be Careful, Little Eyes." Growing up, I remember always singing this song or some version of it and shared it with each of my children when they were toddlers. In case you have never heard the song, the lyrics are as follows:

> *O be careful little eyes what you see, O be careful little eyes what you see, there's a Father up above and He's looking down in love so, be careful little eyes what you see*
>
> *O be careful little ears what you hear, O be careful little ears what you hear, there's a Father up above and He's looking down in love so, be careful little ears what you hear*
>
> *O be careful little hands what you do, O be careful little hands*

what you do, there's a Father up above and He's looking down in love so, be careful little hands what you do

O be careful little feet where you go, O be careful little feet where you go, there's a Father up above and He's looking down in love so, be careful little feet where you go

O be careful little mouth what you say, O be careful little mouth what you say, there's a Father up above and He's looking down in love so, be careful little mouth what you say.

—author unknown[3]

Upon further reflection, I realized that *O Be Careful* is a song about mindfulness. For example, if you are using negatives when you speak, you are encouraged to try to convert those negative words and thoughts into positives. So that rather than saying something will not work, think the opposite and consider how it *will* work.

Instead of spending your time fretting about whether a past decision was correct or incorrect, consider your growth potential and close the door on emotional purgatory. Mindfulness and reflection are both empowering strategies to decrease your stress so that you have the opportunity to continue moving away from distress and improve your emotional wellness.

Renewing your purpose. One of my favorite quotes from Florence Nightingale, the founder of modern nursing, is "let whoever is in charge keep this simple question in her head, not how can I always do this right thing myself, but, how can I provide for this right thing to always be done."[4]

For me the meaning behind her words speaks to your legacy. Sometimes the best opportunity to grow after loss is to renew your purpose by focusing on helping and advocating for others. Dr. Martin

Luther King said that "whatever affects one directly, affects all indirectly. . . . This is the interrelated structure of reality."[5] Therefore, it is important that you understand that your outreach does not have to be a major undertaking; a small action could ignite a change that impacts the world.

Self-actualization. Self-actualization may not seem achievable in the midst of your distress, yet, if you think about it in terms of opening yourself to inner peace, it is not only possible but probable. Consider how you might take small steps to live your life to the fullest potential starting today and moving forward. Perhaps there is something that you have wanted to do; it could be very small, like committing to fishing once a week or spending your downtime taking a nap in the afternoon. Or taking a hot bath every night. Or maybe you would like to make a major life change, such as changing your career, downsizing your home, or pursing a long-term educational goal. Having a plan that includes both short-term stress relievers and long-term goals that you plan to achieve over time is a major step so that you can ultimately achieve self-actualization.

My husband and his siblings worked tirelessly to ensure that the needs of their father were met and continue to work to ensure that their mother is being cared for, but it has been tremendously stressful. Because we are all under such strain, it was important that we discuss how to recognize the symptoms associated with developing a stress disorder.

What worked best for our family, and what you may find helpful as well, is to ensure that you take the time to preemptively implement healthy ways to cope with and work through symptoms of stress and distress. It is beneficial to identify your potential for a post-traumatic response so that you are empowered under what can be complicated circumstances.

Even though they are sad, Terrence and his siblings feel blessed because they still have one another; in addition, we are all encouraged to reach out and access additional resources should the need arise. I hope that you, too, are emboldened to reach out should you feel that you need assistance to alleviate your feelings of distress.

Acknowledge your feelings

Take a moment to document a life event that you find distressing and that you are in the midst of now.

_____
_____
_____
_____
_____

Do you need to separate yourself from old ways?

_____
_____
_____
_____
_____

How does fear or anxiety affect your level of confidence during tough days?

_____
_____
_____
_____
_____

Take a moment to document one small practice and one long-term goal that you can use to cope when you are distressed.

_____
_____
_____
_____
_____

Stay open to being Inspired

Sometimes we make the process more complicated than we need to. We will never make a journey of a thousand miles by fretting about how long it will take or how hard it will be. We make the journey by taking each day step by step and then repeating it again and again until we reach our destination.

—Joseph Wirthlin[6]

Reflect deeply so that you can heal

Be mindful. Take time to reflect. Be open to embracing change even when you do not fully understand. Take time to consider your potential growth. Always be open to learning from your experiences. When possible, try to avoid analysis paralysis, but take time to make informed decisions. Then, do not dwell on what has already happened; rather, stay open to growing from the experience, and by all means, share all that you have learned.

---

[1] Christopher McCandless. (n.d.). BrainyQuote.com. http://www.brainyquote.com/quotes/authors/c/christopher_mccandless.html, access February 12, 2016

[2] Alan Watts. BrainyQuote.com, Xplore Inc, 2016. http://www.brainyquote.com/quotes/authors/a/alan_watts.html, accessed July 8, 2016.

[3] Author unknown. (nd). O be Careful, Little Mouth. Timeless Truths Free Online Library. http://library.timelesstruths.org/texts/Treasures_of_the_Kingdom_49/Be_Careful_Little_Eyes/, accessed September 29, 2016.

[4] Florence Nightingale (1969). Notes on Nursing: What It Is, and What It Is Not. Dover Publications. Mineola: NY.

[5] Martin Luther King, Jr.. BrainyQuote.com, Xplore Inc, 2016. http://www.brainyquote.com/quotes/quotes/m/martinluth403521.html, accessed May 24, 2016.

[6] Joseph B. Wirthlin. (n.d.). BrainyQuote.com. http://www.brainyquote.com/quotes/authors/j/joseph_b_wirthlin.html, accessed on February 12, 2016

The Empty Chair Prayer

When I cried, someone comforted me. When I worried, someone soothed me. When I panicked, someone prayed for me. When I felt alone, someone hugged me. When I wanted to give up, someone said, "Hold on, you can make it." For my God has kept his promises to me. He promised to wipe away all of my tears, and he did. He promised never to leave me and forsake me, and He didn't. What a mighty God I serve!!!

—Linda Joy, 2001

I have always loved public speaking, but praying out loud or in front of a group, not so much. Perhaps the source of my apprehension with sharing my personal devotion in public is that I have little experience with it, or maybe my trepidation originates from the personal belief that, similar to spirituality, prayer in its purest form is a deeply private and highly individualized communion with God or your higher power.

Indeed, I am consistently relieved when Grandma Ella takes the initiative to lead the family in prayer before Sunday dinner and on Thanksgiving. On the other hand, private prayer, silent reflection, and meditation are practices that I find deeply comforting. Indeed, prayer is intrinsic, and although how, when, where, and with whom you pray can vary, depending on your beliefs, it is a natural response when you are distressed.

With regard to prayer, best-selling author and life coach, Iyanla Vanzant expressed that in her deepest, darkest moments, what really got her through was a prayer. She also revealed that "sometimes my prayer was 'Help me.' Sometimes a prayer was 'Thank you.'" But what Iyanla discovered is that intimate connection and communication with her Creator will always get her through because she knows that support and help are just a prayer away.[1]

I find it reassuring to know that I am not alone in the belief that prayers do not need to be elaborate to be effective. Yet, even with the knowledge that your prayers are yours alone, you may find that when you are coping with grief, you are lost for words. The following is a collection of prayers that I have found to be fruitful for my personal healing. You are encouraged to honor one truth, which is that intercession depends on your beliefs and private practices, and therefore every suggested prayer may not work for you in its entirety.

In essence, you are encouraged to take the meat and throw away the bones, to use what works and disregard what does not. In fact, I hope that you are emboldened to customize and integrate components of the prayers that speak to you personally as you work through your sadness.

TWO PRAYERS FOR YOUR LOVED ONE

The Mourner's Prayer

The mourner's Kaddish is a tradition of linking your personal grief with the collective grief of the Jewish people referred to in the Bible.[2] Kaddish is recited three times a day for a year during community prayer, in a fashion similar to the call and response that is often a part of Sunday benediction in most churches.

The prayer of Kaddish

May His great Name grow exalted and sanctified, in the world that He created as He willed?

May He give reign to His kingship in your lifetimes and in your days, and in the lifetimes of the entire Family of Israel, swiftly and soon?

Amen.

May His great Name be blessed forever and ever?

Blessed, praised, glorified, exalted, extolled, mighty, upraised, and lauded be the Name of the Holy One, Blessed is He beyond any blessing and song, praise and consolation that are uttered in the world.

Amen.

May there be abundant peace from Heaven, and life upon us and upon all Israel.

Amen.

He who makes peace in His heights, May He make peace, upon us and upon all Israel.

Amen.[3]

You may have noticed that there are no specific references to grief within the supplication. You are correct, as Kaddish does not speak to bereavement directly; rather, according to Rabbi Bernard Lipnick,[4] it addresses three obstacles that mourners must commonly overcome.

The first hurdle relates to the potential loss of faith and/or a questioning of faith, the second difficulty is the query associated with the brevity of life and why we are here in the first place, and the third questions why we have to die.

If you recall, my mother's faith was shattered as a result of my aunt Linda's passing. A particular sticking point for my mom was trying to rationalize mortality: first my aunt's and then her own. This questioning became a major source of distress, and she took a considerable amount of time pondering the meaning of life and death.

Although my mother is not a student of Judaism, I think that by understanding the meaning of Kaddish, she would have more comfortably adopted Rabbi Lipnick's conclusion that God created a world according to divine will, in which death is the inevitable, but that it is imperative that you embrace the fact that you have a mission while you are here.

I do not suggest that my mom's feelings of sadness would have dissipated simply by saying the Kaddish. To the contrary, what I am suggesting is that having an understanding of the prayer, its meaning and historical context, would have reassured my mother that the spiritual questioning in her grief was both natural and necessary for her healing.

The Empty Chair Prayer

Based on psychologist Fredrick Pearl's and Gestalt therapy, the "empty chair" is a counseling technique that has been found to be particularly useful when grief is complicated. Through guided therapy, you are encouraged to openly express any unresolved issues between you and your loved one who has passed.

There is a traditional method wherein the therapist facilitates a discussion between you and your loved one through a series of interviews and guided exercises. There is also an approach where psychodrama is used and you are invited to play the role of yourself and your loved one lost by physically exchanging your position from one chair to another. The ultimate goal of the exercise is to release any unresolved feelings associated with your loss by saying anything that you feel may have been left unsaid.

Similar to the empty chair counseling technique, the empty chair prayer is an approach that you may find useful working through what may be unresolved feelings associated with multiple losses, but the free expression of your feelings rather than resolving complicated grief is the focus. Using an empty chair and luggage tags (or something of your choosing), each family member is encouraged to write down a special remembrance or an antidote about a loved one who is now passed.

Participants are invited to share what was written on the tag by reading the contents aloud and then to pin their tags onto the chair. At the end of the experience, you may appoint someone who is comfortable with praying aloud and encourage him or her to lead the family in prayer. The resulting prayer then becomes original and specific to your family and a part of your legacy totem. It can be a very healing experience.

THREE PRAYERS FOR YOUR PERSONAL HEALING

A prayer for opening doors

In his book, Charles Allen shared a story that I think translates nicely into a prayer. He writes of a man he knows who puts his keys into one of his shoes each night before bed:

> When he awakens each day he says a prayer that goes like this, "lord, this day I will come to certain doors that are locked but I shall use these keys to open those doors. And may I remember this day that there is a key to every situation, a solution to every problem. May I never surrender to one of life's locked doors, instead may I use the keys on the key ring of prayer until the right key and the door be opened.[5]

The story regarding opening doors is a reminder that you hold the keys to your personal healing. I am by no means saying that you should go at it alone, but what I am suggesting is that others do not know how you are feeling unless you are willing to share. There are a variety of ways that you can open the door to release any hidden sadness. This may mean that you pray, meditate, and lean on your social network to work through your sadness.

The Lord's Prayer of the Old Testament

Often referred to as the Lord's Prayer of the Old Testament, the focus of this intercession is to grant you the gift of wholeness and wellness:

> *The LORD bless you and keep you; the LORD make his face shine upon you and be gracious to you; the LORD turn his face toward you and give you peace.*
>
> *—Numbers 6:24–26 NIV*[6]

In his commentary, Mathew Henry suggests that to pray this prayer is "to be under the almighty protection of God our Savior; to enjoy his favor as the smile of a loving Father, or as the cheering beams of the sun; while he mercifully forgives our sins, supplies our wants, consoles the heart, and prepares us by his grace for eternal glory; these things form the substance of this blessing, and the sum total of all blessings. In so rich a list of mercies worldly joys are not worthy to be mentioned."[7]

Even before I knew that this prayer was considered the Lord's Prayer, it was one of my favorite supplications. It seems to apply to so many situations and it is easy for me to remember and recite.

Mindfulness

As a part of the Gita, this Hindu prayer highlights the importance of mindfulness, particularly with regard to the moral struggles that you likely face while grieving:

> Perfection is characterized by one's ability to see the self by the pure mind and to relish and rejoice in the self. In that joyous state, one is situated in boundless spiritual happiness, realized through transcendental senses. Established thus, one never departs from the truth, and upon gaining this he thinks there is no greater gain. Being so situated, one is never shaken even in the midst of greatest difficulty. This indeed is actual freedom from all miseries arising from material contact.
>
> Bhagavad-Gita 6.20–23[8]

For me, this prayer confirms that you are the author of the narratives of your deeply personal pilgrimage that guides your beliefs and values, as evidenced by the choices you make to heal each day.

Saint Teresa of Ávila says that "mental prayer in my opinion is nothing else than an intimate sharing between friends; it means taking time frequently to be alone with Him who we know loves us. The important thing is not to think much but to love much and so do that which best stirs you to love. Love is not great delight but desire to please God in everything."[9]

Perhaps like me you prefer private devotion and silent reflection, or you may be more like Grandma Ella, who is a natural orator of the Green family's collective intercessions. Remember that it is not the approach that matters, but that you have the opportunity for reprieve and spiritual communion in your grief by taking refuge in your prayers.

Acknowledge your feelings

Is there a prayer that brings you comfort that you might document here in your journal?

_____
_____
_____

How about a poem of special meaning that you might include here for encouragement?

_____
_____
_____

Stay open to being Inspired

Try to feel the need for prayer often during the day and take the trouble to pray. Prayer makes the heart large enough until it can contain God's gift of Himself.

—Mother Teresa[10]

Reflections from the Soul

Reflect deeply so that you can heal

Peace be unto you, that which is hidden will soon shine through. Find inner silence where life is quiet and still, traquility is your gift. You have earned inner peace. Enjoy the serenity that only inner peace can bring.

—Dr. Eboni Green

---

[1] Iyanla Vanzant. (n.d.). BrainyQuote.com. http://www.brainyquote.com/quotes/authors/i/iyanla_vanzant.html, accessed February 12, 2016.

[2] Edward Alexander (1999). Saying Kaddish. Judaism, 48 (4), p 420-427.

[3] *Tracey R Rich. (1988-2011). Mourner's Kaddish.*

http://www.jewfaq.org/kaddishref.htm, accessed on July 5, 2016.

[4] Rabbi Bernard Lipnick. (2003). Ron Wolfson. A Time to Mourn, A Time to Comfort *(Jewish Lights)*. As cited in Kaddish speaks to mourners http://www.jewishlights.com, *accessed July 4, 2016.*

[5] Charles Allen. (1977). All things are possible through prayer. Pillar Publishing, Ireland: Dublin.

[6] Bhagavad-gita 4.9, 5.19, 5.24, 8.05. Educational Services (2014). *The heart of Hinduism.* http://iskconeducationalservices.org/HoH/concepts/106.htm, accessed July 5, 2016

[7] Thomas Nelson, *The NKJV Study Bible*, 2nd ed. (Harper Publishing :Nashville, TN 2007), *Numbers 6:24-26.*

[8] Mathew Henry's Commentary, Bible Hub (2016). http://biblehub.com/commentaries/mhc/numbers/6.htm, accessed July 5, 2016.

[9] Saint Teresa of Avila. BrainyQuote.com, Xplore Inc, 2016. http://www.brainyquote.com/quotes/quotes/s/saintteres586959.html, accessed July 5, 2016.

[10] Mother Teresa. (2016). Mother Teresa Quotes. http://www.goodreads.com/author/quotes/838305.Mother_Teresa, accessed July 5, 2016.

The Myth of Closure

It feels like forever and a day since I saw your warm and tender face, the smile you expressed, your style, your grace. The way you entered a room and made heads turn in a way that only you could. It seems like forever and a day since I held you close and felt your warm embrace. Since you held me tightly in your arms and gave me comfort, the type of comfort that only you could give. It could be forever and a day and I would not forget how you impacted my life, how you made me a better person, how you supported me throughout the years, how you encouraged me when no one else would. That you loved me, that I love you—even though you are no longer here with me. It feels like, it seems like, it could be, forever and a day. . .

—Dr. Eboni Ivory Green

Conventional wisdom suggests that after loss, you will succinctly progress through the five stages of grief, and then after about a year, the weight of your sadness will be lifted so that you can achieve closure. However, if you are like most grieving caregivers, you will find that fixing your mind on obtaining closure is similar to attempting to hit a moving target from a thousand miles away.

The truth is that concept of closure in grief is poorly conceived. Yet, because it is a term that has been broadly applied in grief work, you may feel as though you have failed in some way if you are not able to close the door on your sadness.

For me, the myth was shattered when my mother and I embarked on a pilgrimage to New York a few years after my grandmother's passing. The culmination of our journey was to place a special locket containing her ashes with my grandfather by his tombstone and to reunite the rest of her remains in the family plot with her father, mother, and brother.

I do not know what we were expecting to happen, but in retrospect, I recognize that I was operating on the assumption that at the end of the trip, my mother and I would have closure. I believed with all my heart, as did my mom, that the collective weight of our grief would be lifted immediately.

But when we arrived at my grandmother's final resting place and I did not have an emotional release, I was dismayed. It was not until I started writing this book that my mother shared that she had felt the same. For this reason, I began to reframe the concept of closure and to welcome the idea of working toward homeostasis in grief.

In the opening section "Riptides of Sadness," the idea of homeostasis in grief is introduced as a concept that places emphasis on acknowledging your pain so that you can identify and implement coping strategies that are specific to you personally. Postulating homeostasis as an alternative to closure is purposeful so that you are reminded that you will likely experience sadness, remember special things about your loved one, and tackle your heartache in some way for the rest of your life.

The good news is that you have the opportunity to acknowledge the impact your loved one had on your life and to remember what you loved best about your relationship. It is hopeful that you work to integrate your past and present feelings about your loved one so that you are able to reinvest your emotions into living.

FOUR PRACTICES THAT PROMOTE HOMEOSTASIS WHILE GRIEVING

Acknowledge the impact your loved one had on your life. Take a moment to identify two or three ways that your loved one has impacted your life. Perhaps your loved one was patient or wise, had a sense of dedication to family and friends, or was someone who had the ability to lighten your mood simply by walking into the room. Is there something that you learned that can be incorporated into your daily life?

For example, if your loved one made sure the family stayed connected, is it possible that you could be instrumental by stepping in to assume that role? Maintaining a symbolic bond with your loved one who has passed is a healthy way to recognize the significant role that he or she has had on whom you are today. What is most important is that, whatever you do, it is authentic to you and contributes to your well-being.

Try writing an epitaph to memorialize your loved one. Identify a special characteristic about your loved one. The goal is to take your time so that you have the opportunity to truly reflect, and then, when you are ready, try writing something that represents the relationship you and your loved one shared. This could be documented in an epitaph where you create a phrase or expression to memorialize your lost loved one. You may choose to share it or keep it private, and from time to time, you might benefit from revisiting your epitaph as a way to remember your loved one.

Do not be afraid to acknowledge that your life has changed. Without intending it, you may share a specific line of thinking, similar mannerisms, and/or values as someone who has held a significant place in your life. As you may recall, Cynthia was my favorite aunt; she had a magnetic personality and loved to laugh. When she died, I was devastated and wasn't sure how I would cope. Yet having time to reflect helped me recognize that we continue to have a relationship, because, through her humor, she left a strong life imprint. I believe that every life leaves an imprint.

The following questions might be helpful as you document your loved one's life imprint. You should not feel pressured to think of your responses quickly. In fact, please take your time.

What impact did your loved one have on your life?

What would you like to affirm or maintain?

What would you like to relinquish or change?

Once you feel comfortable with your answers, you are encouraged to put the list aside for a while. Later you might revisit it and revise your answers so that you can determine how to integrate your loved one's imprint into your daily life.

There is always the possibility that you will see your loved one again. Perhaps not in the literal sense, but in your dreams, when you look at your family, a family pet, or when you commune with nature. When you are feeling safe enough emotionally, it is important to take time to go to places and to be around people who remind you of your loved one. I am a firm believer that your loved ones live on through the stories shared about them; the more you share, the longer they are remembered and stay living in your heart and mind.

It is important that you be cautious of listening to the suggestion that the goal of grief work is to find closure, that you should only experience sadness briefly, and that you will then close the door on your sadness and return to normal. This is simply not true. Loss changes you. Rather than placing pressure on yourself to arbitrarily move through stages, free yourself so that you have the opportunity to do what works best for your very personal pilgrimage of grief.

Acknowledge your feelings

Take some time to review your journal entries. What have you learned about yourself from reading your journal entries?

_____
_____
_____
_____
_____

How can you use what you are learning to help you move forward?

_____
_____
_____
_____
_____

Are there any events that have caused you pain that you are avoiding but that may ultimately bear the fruit of understanding?

_____
_____
_____
_____
_____

Are there some lessons you thought you had learned and then forgot to apply in your life that caused history to repeat itself?

_____
_____
_____
_____
_____
_____

Part Three: What About Your Grieving Family?

So He sent my family to care for me because we were in the same place spiritually and could support one another. We had lost a son, a nephew, an aunt, an uncle, a mother, a grandmother, a sister, and a brother. Our collective losses brought clarity and shined a light on what is truly important in life, FAMILY!

—Dr. Eboni Green

God Sets the Lonely in Families

If our hearts are ready for anything, we can be open to our inevitable losses, and to the depths of our sorrow. We can grieve our lost loves, our lost youth, our lost health, and our lost capacities. This is part of our humanness, part of the expression of our love for life.

—Tara Brach[1]

Grandma Ella lost three sons in a matter of a few short years. She lost her oldest son, Willie, after he suffered from a massive heart attack. Shortly thereafter her two younger sons, Andy and Michael, both died from complications associated with chronic illnesses. Grandma was the caregiver for all three sons, each of whom died before reaching forty.

The tragic losses of Willie, Michael, and Andy altered the family dynamics. The truth is that caring for, and then losing, someone you love can place a significant strain on both you and your family. Although the pain associated with grief is not unique to caring families, the pain you feel often differs from the pain of those who did not share in the unique experience of both having cared for and lost a loved one.

It is important to recognize that the strain of loss can impede effective communication among family members, hindering the ability to support one another and complicating your ability to work through feelings of grief. In fact, when just one relative experiences complicated grief, the resulting crisis can have a ripple effect on the entire family.

Coping mechanisms and communication styles are interrupted. This is why it is important to recognize that each of your family members will inevitably process grief differently. For example, it is important to consider the life experiences, position, or station of your loved one who has passed (i.e., patriarch or matriarch), the closeness of the relationship, and any unresolved conflicts that can influence both your and your relatives' grief responses.

Therefore, it is imperative to understand the differences and similarities in how you and your family members process grief. Explore what influences each person's grief, as well as how they express their feelings of sadness so that you are each empowered to support one another.

WHAT IS INFLUENCING YOUR GRIEF?

Life Experiences

Life experiences play a role in shaping perceptions about the world, including those about death. In my opinion, past experiences associated with the death of a family member or a close friend are a crucial component of how death is processed. For example, when I was ten or eleven, a teenage girl who attended my grandmother's church was brutally murdered. When she died, my cousins and I were made to attend the wake service. It was an unsettling experience and a horrible way to fully come to terms with my own mortality.

Years later, while I was training to become a nursing assistant, I cared for a young girl who was extremely ill. One day, she quietly passed away. The nursing assistant skillfully balanced caring for the deceased body of the sweet young girl, with comforting me as an individual who had never tended to a person after death.

I share this life experience with you to illustrate the traumatic way in which I became aware of my own mortality, in contrast to the tender way in which I learned to professionally care for those patients nearing the end of life. I do not think I would be as passionate about caregiving if I had not been trained by such a caring nursing assistant.

Position or Station

The position or station (i.e., patriarch or matriarch) an individual holds in the family can influence the way grief is processed. As previously mentioned, Willie was the patriarch of the Green family, becoming a father figure for his four younger siblings. Later, Willie, a successful businessman, also assumed the role of provider. Everyone in the family depended on him for something, and losing him was devastating.

When a loved one suffers from a chronic or terminal illness, there is the opportunity to gradually redistribute roles over an extended period of time. However, Willie suffered a sudden heart attack, and there was no time for family members to make adjustments. Roles had to be redefined immediately, since the family was simultaneously working through feelings of acute grief, as well as the loss of their patriarch.

The Personal Relationship

Family members are in a unique position to have a level of intimacy with each other that may not be experienced in any other relationship. Being a caregiver for a loved one provides an additional layer of intimacy as traditional roles (i.e., husband, wife, son, daughter) are reversed. The intensity of grief experienced following the loss of a loved one is proportionate to the intensity of the love shared in the relationship.

Factors such as the level of emotional support, financial security, and degree of companionship provided in the relationship are equally important considerations when it comes to how you process the loss of a loved one. Some caregivers not only face living alone for the first time, but find that old friendships and other sources of support are greatly diminished as a result of a long-term commitment to caring for a loved one.

In addition to these changes, you may also face the following adjustments: the termination of services and supports needed to care for your loved one; reluctance in sharing your loss with support groups where other members are still active caregivers; and the shifting of your identity from "I am a caregiver" to "I was a caregiver."

Each of these adjustments generally occurs within a short period of time, usually days or weeks. The end result is that you may feel isolated at a time when you need to rely on your family and social network for support. If one takes a closer look at the loss of personal relationships in conjunction with the loss of a loved one, it is not hard to conclude that loneliness is a common feeling among grieving caregivers and their families.

Everyone Hurts

YOUR GRIEVING FAMILY MEMBERS

How Family Members Express their Sadness.

Everyone hurts, but may express his or her sadness in a unique manner. Understanding common responses to grief enhances your ability to support relatives. It is important to understand as much as possible right away, so that positive communication begins early and behaviors remain consistent, leading to improved interactions.

The following paragraphs outline ten common emotional responses to grief. They may assist you in better understanding how to communicate with, and comfort your grieving family. The ten emotional responses include:

- The Connector,
- The Boundary Tester,
- Overcome by Grief,
- The Blamer,
- Lost in Action,
- On a Rampage,
- Simply Overwhelmed,

- The Voice of Reason,
- The Rock,
- The Comforter.

These characteristics are not all-encompassing, as there are a wide range of ways in which individuals cope with grief. Strategies that best support each family member are also included. Please take a moment to review how your relatives might react to loss of a loved one, and how you can best support one another.

The Connector

The connector is usually the most socially networked family member. He or she has access to family members' contact information, is fairly organized, and is a good communicator. Connectors are resourceful and can diffuse high-tension situations. They usually know when to use what strategy with whom, and may use differences between individual family members for the benefit of the family. Grandma is the connector in the Green family. She pulled the family members closer after Willie, Michael, and Andy each passed away. Grandma stayed in contact with Willie's and Michael's daughters and remains the center connection for the family.

Whenever there is a family gathering, Grandma is usually the organizer. The connector is a valuable resource to the family. If you have a family member who is a connector, do not be afraid to step back and allow him or her to take the lead in planning family events and smoothing the waters during difficult times.

The Boundary Tester

Some family members are more inclined to test boundaries than others. The boundary tester in your family may have possessed the ability to test individuals throughout life. His or her grief may serve to intensify that need, to ask unanswerable questions interjecting when there is no need in an effort to get a response. Later, when everyone is frustrated, the boundary tester may sit on the sidelines to watch the fireworks. It is important to recognize that he or she is expressing raw emotion in the only way they know. Try not to exert much energy when a loved one is testing boundaries. Do not be afraid to be firm, set limits, and then move on.

Overcome by Grief

Some of your relatives may be overcome by grief and might physically demonstrate it by wailing, collapsing, pulling their hair, screaming, or crying. More reserved family members may feel uncomfortable at this reaction. It is important to consider that we cannot always relate to what another is feeling. Try to be understanding and nonjudgmental. If you have a relative who is overcome by grief, consider offering a quiet presence, or a comforting touch. Do not be afraid to allow your loved one to express sadness through tears and raw emotion. The comfort you provide may contribute to improved well-being for that relative.

The Blamer

A friend lost his father after a long-term battle with cancer. One of his relatives immediately went on the offense, blaming and criticizing others in the family. Caregivers already worn down by the very nature of losing a loved one can find themselves the target of personal attacks. The blamer needs a scapegoat on whom to misdirect anger, because to the blamer, everything that has transpired is someone else's fault. Comments made by a blamer are generally inappropriate and unproductive. No one wants to be assaulted with negative energy, so, recognize the blaming for what it is—an attempt to control and make others as upset as the blamer is. Try not to take it personally.

Lost in Action

Years ago, I worked with a person who became the full-time caregiver for her mother following her father's death. She shared how her brother came into town for her father's funeral, but did not help with the arrangements, and was unavailable to help her with her mother who needed full-time care. There are some family members who are less available than others. This relative may prefer solitude and time to reflect, as opposed to being surrounded by people.

The isolation may be associated with the lack of coping skills to deal with the situation. Distance does not necessarily indicate that this family member cares any less than others, but it can be frustrating just the same. If you have a relative who is lost in action, ask him or her directly for the support you need. Make sure your request is directly tied to a specific action, and based on a time line. If it is possible for you get the task done without the assistance of this family member, do so.

On a Rampage

Feelings of frustration and helplessness following the loss of a loved one can be outwardly expressed as anger. The anger may not be felt for a particular individual, but similar to the blamer's style, is frequently projected onto family members who are not the source of the tension.

Anger may also be directed at relatives who are perceived to have even minimally participated in the care of a loved one. In our grief, we sometimes judge family members based on unrealistically high standards. When expectations are unreasonable, disappointment is the inevitable result. Usually the relative on a rampage is by nature an individual with an intolerant personality.

Directing anger inward is also possible, and could represent the loss of control over the lives of the deceased and close family members. When a loved one is on a rampage, it is important to avoid offering him or her advice, as it is unlikely that they will appreciate it. Do not react directly to the anger, but allow your relative to vent. Try to keep in mind that the anger is due to the loss. If you are unable to keep your temper with a loved one on a rampage, try connecting him or her to the voice of reason.

Simply Overwhelmed

Several years before my grandmother passed away, she lost her best friend. For some time following the loss, she described her thoughts as scattered and her feelings as indecisive. My grandmother was simply overwhelmed.

An overwhelmed family member is unable to process the many emotions associated with grief. He or she knows the loved one has passed, however, there is difficulty with returning to normalcy, and this person needs reassurance. The individual's memory may also be faulty during this period, so try to discuss only one issue at a time. Sticking to a routine and being a good listener can also be ways to support an overwhelmed loved one.

The Voice of Reason

The voice of reason is usually the patriarch or matriarch of the family. He or she can also be someone who is now assuming a leadership role for the first time following the death of a loved one. If bickering arises, the voice of reason seeks to identify the real issues. This family member is skilled with getting to the core issues causing family tension and works swiftly to get them resolved. The voice of reason is generally a good listener. He or she may broaden perspectives. When conflicts arise within the family, seek out the voice of reason.

The Rock

The rock is usually a male family member who is in a leadership or patriarchal position. The rock may have conflicted feelings resulting from the need to be strong for others, while simultaneously coping with his own loss. He or she may not feel allowed to openly express personal grief in front of everyone. The rock may be given little support, although he or she is expected to be a tower of strength. It is important not to overlook the rock, as this person has the tendency to hold in emotions. Encourage him or her to share feelings openly with the family, or privately with a select few.

The Comforter

The comforter in the family is an individual who makes it easy for others to express their feelings. He or she has no problem allowing you to cry or reminisce. The comforter is a good communicator who always knows just what to say. He or she may also be the person in the family who holds a firm belief in God, and can offer scriptures or other spiritual resources to help you pull through (sometimes the comforter may be a member of the clergy). The comforter may be an individual who calls you just to pray, or to allow you to vent. He or she may also send you an encouraging note or e-mail from time to time. The comforter's calm reassurance is needed, and often greatly appreciated by grieving family members.

The loss of a loved one can result in your relatives coping with a whirlwind of emotions. The differences in how one family member copes with grief versus another can impact your current relationships, and if your grief goes unresolved, those of future generations. Each person processes grief in his or her own time and own way. Therefore, it is impossible to be aware of every emotion your family members are struggling with. Yet it is possible to empathize, by acknowledging that each individual is entitled to his or her feelings, taking care that your responses are measured, and making an honest effort to support one another.

FAMILY CONFLICTS

Even when you are mindful of your relatives' grief responses, the potential for conflict still exists and is even likely. Virginia Satir states, "feelings of worth can flourish only in an atmosphere where individual differences are appreciated, mistakes are tolerated, communication is open, and rules are flexible—the kind of atmosphere that is found in a nurturing family."[2]

My father-in-law was an avid outdoorsman. He relocated from Nebraska to Aberdeen, South Dakota, so he could enjoy what he loved most, fishing and hunting. A few years ago, experiencing a toothache, he went to the dentist, however, having waited so long to make the appointment, his tooth had become infected. The dentist sent him home with a prescription for an antibiotic.

When he did not take the antibiotic as prescribed, the infection traveled through his blood stream and shut down his vital organs. He was transported to a regional hospital and placed on life support.

When we arrived at the hospital, we learned that a close relative had suggested to the health care team that he be removed from life support. The family member said my father-in-law would not want any life-saving procedures. The situation was further complicated because my father-in-law was unresponsive when he arrived at the hospital, he did not have his wishes in writing, and there was no documented next of kin. It took several days for the social workers to contact my husband, and fortunately, he was able to communicate that his father did want treatment. He recovered from the coma.

Later we learned that the same relative who suggested he be taken off life support, took my father-in-law's valuables while he was in the hospital. There was a great deal of tension in the family following this incident. Sometimes tensions and misunderstandings arise as a result of the complex nature of the caregiving situation. In other instances, family conflicts have nothing to do with caregiving, but stem from previous challenges in the relationship with your relative. Marsha Norman writes, "family is just an accident.... They don't mean to get on your nerves. They don't even mean to be your family, they just are."[3]

To put it plainly, a blood relationship does not guarantee that family members will get along. Family conflicts can and often do impact the way grief is processed. When there is a history of family conflict, grief can create distance between family members, or it can bring them together.

Grief as a Distancing Emotion within the Family

Grief can create distance between family and friends. Sometimes the distance is used as a form of self-preservation, creating space as a protective mechanism. This space shelters you from expressing, or even fully experiencing, the overwhelming feelings associated with the death of your loved one. Sometimes the disease from which your loved one suffered promotes distancing.

For example, Alzheimer's disease can be especially distancing, as it is emotionally challenging to watch your loved one steadily decline both physically and mentally. This was how many relatives reacted when my grandmother, Gran, was diagnosed with Alzheimer's. When she died, it was so devastating that some family members just wanted to be left alone for a while. Some did not feel comfortable, or simply were not ready to express their sadness openly with the rest of the family.

The good news is that after a time, family naturally comes back together—most of the time. According to Mignon McLaughlin, "family quarrels have a total bitterness unmatched by others. Yet it sometimes happens that they also have a kind of tang, a pleasantness beneath the unpleasantness, based on the tacit understanding that this is not for keeps; that any limb you climb out on will still be there later for you to climb back."[4]

In our family a little distance was healthy, and actually served to preserve relationships, as each individual had the opportunity to process his or her feelings prior to the next family gathering.

Grief as a Connector Bridge within the Family

Many families are geographically separated, and sometimes lose contact with one another. On the other hand, some of your family members might live in the same city, yet find it difficult to get together simply because your lives are filled with responsibilities and commitments. Grief can pull the family together, as relatives reach out to one another after a loved one has passed away. Because grief is a social process, there is an unspoken need for families to grieve together, to talk about the circumstances surrounding the death of a loved one, and to support one another.

There are numerous strategies that can be implemented to bring your family together after your loved one has passed away. Perhaps you might try to put together a Chinese lantern ceremony as described in the chapter, "The Transfer of Hope" or the empty chair prayer outlined in the chapter, "The Empty Chair Prayer" each of which has been found to be cathartic for grieving families. The idea is that you identify productive ways to release your feelings of sadness, while spending time with your family.

Creating a Family Totem

Novelist Eden Robinson has written extensively about the power of the totem and says, "Not so long ago, the bay was lined with longhouses and canoes, totem poles and fishing gear. The reserve was once a winter village, a place to celebrate the sacred season, when memories passed in dance and song, and stories from one generation to the next, with great feasts called potlatches."[5]

Prior to writing this chapter, my knowledge of a family totem did not extend beyond what was introduced in the Disney movie *Brother*

Bear. Like most, I thought of it as a religious relic, but a totem is really a representation of your family history.

The practice of building a totem is attributed to the aboriginal peoples. You and your family might create one as a way to highlight important family events and share traditions and stories about family members.

To begin, you might set a time so that the family can get together and take a few moments to sketch out a totem pole that represents the story of your family, including a loved one who has passed. Then take special care to describe your loved one's life story, highlighting those symbols that represent the significant points that you remember of the two of you together. Next try writing out a story that describes the symbolic images on paper. It may take more than one gathering to truly capture your full family history. Creating a totem can be a cleansing activity while also communicating your familial legacy.

I leave you with this final thought, expressed by Thomas Moore, regarding the nature of family. "Family life is full of major and minor crises—the ups and downs of health, success and failure in career, marriage, and divorce—and all kinds of characters. It is tied to places and events and histories. With all of these felt details, life etches itself into memory and personality. It's difficult to imagine anything more nourishing to the soul."[6]

Moore's words get to the crux of what it means to have relatives on which you can depend. You may not always get along, but deep within you share a common and unbreakable bond for one another. Because after all, you are family.

---

[1] Tara Brach. BrainyQuote.com, Xplore Inc, 2016. https://www.brainyquote.com/quotes/quotes/t/tarabrach528159.html, accessed September 29, 2016.

[2] Virginia Satir. BrainyQuote.com, Xplore Inc, 2016. https://www.brainyquote.com/quotes/quotes/v/virginiasa175186.html, accessed September 29, 2016.

[3] Marsha Norman. GoodReads.com. http://www.goodreads.com/quotes/236806-family-is-just-accident-jessie-it-s-nothing-personal-hon-they, accessed September 29, 2016.

[4]Mignon McLaughlin. BrainyQuote.com, Xplore Inc, 2016. https://www.brainyquote.com/quotes/authors/m/mignon_mclaughlin.html, accessed September 29, 2016.

[5]Eden Robinson. BrainyQuote.com, Xplore Inc, 2016. https://www.brainyquote.com/quotes/quotes/e/edenrobins748494.html, accessed September 29, 2016.

[6]Thomas Moore. Searchquotes.com. http://www.searchquotes.com/quotation/Family_life_is_full_of_major_and_minor_crises_-_the_ups_and_downs_of_health%2C_success_and_failure_in/5410/, accessed September 30, 2016.

Epilouge: All in Good Time

I understand that allowing the full reality of this death to enter my head and heart is a source of necessary hurt. While I do not seek the hurt, I seek the healing. Once I understand that, the pain actually begins to dissolve. Yes, I still hurt, but the depth of the pain will ease over time.

—Allen Wolfelt

Dancing Beautifully with a Limp

Whatever life brings you was prepared from all eternity; and the tread of causes was from the beginning of time spinning the fabric of your existence, and every incidental fiber that weaves your web.

—Marcus Aurelius[1]

When my grandmother, Frankie Roberts was a little girl, she was diagnosed with rheumatic fever, a relatively serious illness that led to crippling valvular heart disease. She experienced excessive fatigue, heart palpitations, and shortness of breath, and was so weak physically that most of her time was spent shut away inside. The resulting intense isolation she endured forced her to search for the meaning and purpose of life by leaning on her faith.

In the early 1940s, she attended the Harlem School of Nursing, became a registered nurse, married my grandfather, and had four beautiful daughters, the youngest of whom was my mother. When the girls became adults, my grandmother decided to go on a medical mission to Panama City. Needing to stay awake, she took a medication similar to NoDoz®, and her heart, already weakened from rheumatic heart disease, started to pump inadequately.

The doctor decided to stop and then restart my grandmother's heart to regulate the rhythm, an action that only served to further weaken her heart. I was with her on a missionary trip in Mississippi when her heart stopped beating a second time. Emergency open heart surgery was immedately performed, and to save her life, her mitral valve was replaced with an artificial one. She was fifty-three.

A little over twenty years passed. Then one night I received a frantic call from my mom. My grandmother was in the hospital after having suffered another heart attack and then a stroke. The doctor informed us that her artifical heart valve needed to be replaced immediately, and that she would not live more than twenty-four hours without medical intervention. She declined surgery, and against the doctor's orders, was removed from the machines keeping her alive. She lived two more years!

One quiet day in July 2002, my grandmother died. She was sitting at the table, having purchased a new dress and hat, looking at a map and deciding where she would visit next, when she took her last breath. It was the type of quiet, dignified homegoing that she deserved.

I was devastated when my grandmother died. Her passing changed my life and resulted in a spiritual awakening. In an effort to cope, I poured my soul into writing my second book, *At the Heart of the Matter: A Spiritual Journey for Caregivers*. Yet, even in my sadness, I was thankful for the additional two years that she had lived, and I truly believe that God gave her that time to teach me five important lessons.

Although you will find these lessons sprinkled throughout this book, I feel compelled to share them here, in one place, so that their importance is undeniable. Should you experience a time when you are at a loss as to where to begin to address your sadness, I hope that you are empowered to revisit the contents of this book to gain additional insight and renewed strength.

LESSON ONE

People are our roses. My grandmother took this principle to heart, as she never cared much about material things, but always took pride in investing in people. When you learn to give and receive love, acknowledge your truth, and accept others because of, or in spite of, theirs, you have the opportunity to experience true richness in life. Spending time with the people you love, and nurturing the relationships of those whom you hold dear, is vitally important. When you have the opportunity to reflect, having invested in the people you love will likely not be among your regrets.

LESSON TWO

Losing someone you love hurts. The truth is that loss changes you a bit, alters your perspectives, and you will likely work to cope with your feelings of sadness for the rest of your life. *Yet, there is hope that one day the deep sorrow will now take a place in history.*

LESSON THREE

You have a legacy. My grandmother's legacy was for those she loved to learn, understand, accept, and recognize what God has to offer. I continue to work toward fulfilling her legacy in my life, and have adopted the words of John Henry Cardinal Newman as my personal mission statement. He wisely reflects, "God has created me to do God some definite service; He has committed some work to me which He has not committed to another. I have my mission—I never may know it in this life, but I shall be told it in the next.... I am a link in a chain, a bond of connection between persons. God has not created me for naught." [2]

What is your personal mission? I invite you to ponder until you find something that speaks to you, then share it and incorporate it into your life. Perhaps your personal mission will also be a part of your legacy.

LESSON FOUR

Be open to teachable moments. Teachable moments are those times when you are invited to learn a life lesson. They can be either missed opportunities for personal growth or learned life lessons that fill your basket of experiences. Even the most excruciating pain and loss can present an opportunity to grow through personal assessment. No matter how challenging the circumstance, when there is an opportunity to increase human potential, there are lessons to be learned, so stay open.

LESSON FIVE

You may never make sense out of suffering, but you can seek meaning in your journey. Jack Wintz shares, "As humans we will never make total sense out of the mystery of suffering. But we cope with it most sensibly by participating as actively as we can in the healing process, and entrusting ourselves to the supreme source of love and wisdom."[3] I believe this with all my heart.

Much of the suffering witnessed by caregivers in their work simply does not make sense. However, there might be something, whether large or small, that can be gleaned to aid you on your pilgrimage.

The numerous insights gathered after the loss of my grandmother were only apparent when I was able to work through my immediate sadness. Clarity of my feelings did not come easily, and from time to time, I still experience periods of intense grief. Yet I am comforted because I have the opportunity to share the five lessons I learned from my grandmother with you. I hope that you, too, are comforted.

It is my sincere desire that you are encouraged to continuing the tough work of addressing your feelings as they arise. Give yourself permission to tap into raw emotions with the understanding that it is perfectly all right to feel just how you feel today, and each day moving forward. Some of these feelings may be hard to acknowledge; however, it is my belief that healing abounds when challenging circumstances are approached with an open heart and mind.

As Anne Lamott writes, "you will lose someone you can't live without, and your heart will be badly broken, and the bad news is that you never completely get over the loss of your beloved. But this is also the good news. They live forever in your broken heart that doesn't seal back up. And you come through. It's like having a broken leg that never heals perfectly—that still hurts when the weather gets cold, but you learn to dance with the limp."[4]

You are not alone in your grief! You will hurt, but it is my hope that in some small measure Reflections from the Soul encourages you to dance beautifuly— in spite of your limp!

---

[1]Marcus Arilus, Martin Hammond, and Diskin Clay. Meditations. Penguin Classics. 2003.

[2]John Henry Cardinal Newman. Good Reads.com. http://www.goodreads.com/quotes/408029-god-has-created-me-to-do-him-some-definite-service, accessed July 6, 2016

[3]Jack Wintz, CareNotes, One Caring Place, Abby Press: IN

[4]Anne Lamott, "Good Reads.com. http://www.goodreads.com/author/show/7113.Anne_Lamott, accessed July 6, 2016.

About the Author

Dr. Eboni I. Green is a registered nurse and family caregiver. She holds a PhD in human services, with a specialization in health care administration. She currently serves as a professor for the College of Health Sciences, at more than one University where she teaches graduate courses in health care administration. Dr. Green has extensive experience focusing on caregivers' health and wellness, with an emphasis on caregiver stress, burnout, and related family conflicts. In addition, she has contributed to a number of publications and given presentations that focus on training, assessing, and supporting caregivers throughout their caregiving journey. As an accomplished author, Dr. Green has published three books focusing on family caregiving: *At the Heart of the Matter, Caregiving in the New Millennium*, and *Reflections from the Soul*. Please feel free to contact Dr. Eboni I. Green directly to purchase her books, or to schedule trainings, or for national speaking opportunities. Her email address at Caregiver Support Services is: caregiversupport@aol.com or you can accesses her via the Web at ***http://www.caregiversupportservices.org***.

At the Heart of the Matter

Caregivers have unique needs as you provide support and care for your loved ones. At the Heart of the Matter ultimately enables you to look at ways to better care for yourself and enhance your wellness while providing care for your loved one.

At the Heart of the Matter captures the many facets of caring for a loved one and helps us understand ourselves in the process. A must read for all caregivers.

—Kara Von Arx

Caregiving in the New Millennium

Each caregiving situation is unique when it comes to providing assistance and support for another person. Quite frankly it can be downright demanding and stressful. This book is designed to provide you with helpful hints on how to address the conflicts and tensions that will emerge on occasion between the caregiver and the person receiving the care, as well as tensions with other family members impacted by the situation. In these situations the assistance and support of others, access to timely information and resources, and a deep faith are essential to a successful caregiving journey. You are the only you there is. This book will provide you with the information you need when you need it most, and often provide hints and tips on where to start for answers and support.

This book is a wonderful publication designed to provide a breath of fresh air for caregivers everywhere. The caregiver is often overshadowed by the recipient of the care. The caregiver provides physical and emotional support and often needs support themselves. This book provides thoughtful respite and support interlaced with humor. I can't say enough kind words. If you provide care for a homebound relative this is a MUST READ!

—Steven K. Johnson

As a physician and baby boomer, this is absolutely THE best book on the subject of care giving. Clear, concise, excellent references...Dr. Green has really done her homework to make this difficult issue easier for all of us. A++ A must read!!!

—Dr. Laura Torres-Reyes

www.ingramcontent.com/pod-product-compliance
Lightning Source LLC
LaVergne TN
LVHW051557070426
835507LV00021B/2629